The Organ Pipe Cactus

The Southwest Center Series

Joseph C. Wilder, Editor

The Organ Pipe Cactus

David Yetman

THE UNIVERSITY OF ARIZONA PRESS

TUCSON

The University of Arizona Press
© 2006 The Arizona Board of Regents
All rights reserved

Library of Congress Cataloging-in-Publication Data

Yetman, David, 1941–
    The organ pipe cactus / David Yetman.
      p. cm. – (The Southwest Center series)
    Includes bibliographical references and index.
    ISBN-13: 978-0-8165-2541-6 (pbk. : alk. paper)
    ISBN-10: 0-8165-2541-2 (pbk. : alk. paper)
    1. Organpipe cactus—Arizona. 2. Organpipe
cactus–Sonoran Desert. 3. Organ Pipe Cactus
National Monument (Ariz.) I. Title. II. Series.
QK495.C11 Y48 2006
583'.56–dc22

                              2006005783

Publication of this book is made possible in part by a grant
from the Southwest Center of the University of Arizona.

To Dan Bach

Contents

ILLUSTRATIONS

The Organ Pipe Cactus

Where the Organ Pipes Grow

STENOCEREUS THURBERI (Engelm.) Buxb.; *aaqui* (Mayo, Yaqui); *mehueli* (Guarijío); *ool* (Seri); *túpok* (the fruits: Pima Bajo);[1] *tcutcuis* (Tohono O'odham),[2] *chuchuis* (Gila River Pima);[3] *pitaya(o)*, *pitaya(o) dulce* (northern Sonora);* **organ pipe cactus.**

DEEP IN THE DESERT of southwestern Arizona, a lone grocery store and a couple of gas stations mark the junction of two highways along the route to Mexico. One arrives from Phoenix far to the north, the other from Tucson to the east. Southward from Why—the place's name—a black ribbon of undulating pavement fades into the desert scrub. Along this route many thousands of Americans speed their way to and from the Mexican beach town of Rocky Point, Sonora. A few miles toward Mexico from Why, the roadside landscape changes from flat to very rocky, with craggy, volcanic peaks to the east. A solid, subdued sign welcomes the visitor to Organ Pipe

---

* In much historical and contemporary literature, the term *pitahaya* is used to refer to the cactus *Stenocereus thurberi*. After numerous conversations with Mexican botanists and historians, I have chosen to go with the shorter *pitaya*. In spoken Spanish the two terms are indistinguishable. In central and southern Mexico the *pitahaya* (*Hylocereus undatus*) is an epiphytic cactus widely cultivated for its huge edible fruits. In violation of Spanish rules of pronunciation, *pitahaya* is pronounced (English phonetics) pee-tah-HAI-ya.

Cactus National Monument. The roadway dips and climbs slightly, then briefly peaks in a pass cut through ancient flows of black volcanic rock. A few miles farther the first glimpses of Mexico show a land marked by sharply outlined desert hills jutting from vast arid plains.

This is the heart of the Sonoran Desert, different from and richer than deserts anywhere else in the United States—or the world, for that matter. Those whose eyes are not riveted to the highway can pick out, among the legions of great saguaros, palo verdes, and ironwoods, a decidedly new and spectacular hillside plant appearing suddenly on the eastern and southern slopes, a many-armed, semi-high-rise cactus, the organ pipe. Only rarely in Arizona do its branches reach the height of the average saguaro, but occasionally one or two may reach or exceed 20 ft. (6 m). Most of the first organ pipes visible from the highway are half that tall. Within a few miles, a host of these strange, charismatic cacti, some a bit taller, dot the landscape.

For most folk from more temperate parts of the continent, the organ pipe cactus—called *pitaya* or *pitaya dulce* in Sonora, the Mexican state to the south of Arizona—is an odd, intriguing plant. Few North Americans have an opportunity to see it, for in the United States it survives wild only in one corner of a very dry desert, where for nearly five months of the year the heat is memorable and challenging. Each year hopeful immigrants from the south, without papers and desperate for a better life in *el norte*, die of thirst and dehydration attempting to cross the desert on foot. In summer, temperatures of 110°F (43°C) and above are the rule.

The heat blasts your face as though an oven door just opened, so pounding that Seris from not far south in Mexico speak of "the sound of summer heat." For those wise to the ways of the desert and well stocked with water and shade, this baking enclave makes for the best desert. It is so hot for so long that most folk would not dream of lingering. Yet, here alone in the United States can one become familiar with organ pipes as they spring up from rocky slopes, unmistakable and, for the cactophile, unforgettable. To join the organ

pipe during its reproductive rites, one must endure sweat and thirst.

I saw my first organ pipe in 1960 while I was camping in Organ Pipe Cactus National Monument. I concluded that the great cactus—it is large enough to be charismatic even from a distance—was well named, for large individuals appear to have ranks of upright branches or stems reminiscent of a pipe organ.[4] I learned much later that the name was probably attached because the wood of dead cacti resembles individual organ pipes.[5]

I don't recall seeing many charismatic individuals on that first trip. That may have been because the 1950s was a dry decade, testing the resilience of many desert plants. Organ pipes may have been shriveled and languished under the great stress of prolonged drought when I first visited the monument. Since that time, however, the Sonoran Desert climate has been kind to organ pipes. Cold years have been few, and the period from the mid-1960s through the early 1990s was an extremely wet period in recent history. The combination of rather abundant moisture and benign temperatures probably helped the cacti put on noticeable spurts of growth and assume a healthier appearance. Since the mid-1990s, a very dry, hot period has once again tested their mettle.

The organ pipe is one of only three cacti so unusual and so rare that a national preserve has been established to honor and protect it.[6] It joins a very select group of plants—including Joshua trees, redwoods, sequoias, and the South American conifer *Podocarpus*—on which this honor has been conferred. Because the organ pipes barely make it into the United States, the monument was appropriately established where the cactus grows best in this country—abutting the Mexican border. While the cacti are rare in Arizona, motorists crossing the border into Mexico will find that only a few miles to the southeast of the monument organ pipes abound. They are even more common in Sonora than saguaros (*Carnegiea gigantea*) are in Arizona. East along Mexico Highway 2 and then Mexico Highway 15 to the south, organ pipes are part of the landscape for the next 500 mi. (800 km). North of Why, only sharp-eyed spotters can pick them out, a struggling few clinging to the rocky,

Hillside with organ pipes and saguaros, Organ Pipe Cactus National Monument.

south-facing volcanic slopes. North of those few stragglers, they disappear.

A glance at the distribution of these remarkable cacti shows them to be almost accidental visitors north of the border, casual and recent immigrants that have never achieved full citizenship but are in the process of demonstrating their credentials. Outside the Organ Pipe Cactus National Monument in the United States, only a small number of the plants can be found. These are scattered on a few desert ranges in western Pima and southwestern Pinal Counties in Arizona: an organ pipe here and another there a ridge or so away. Most of them not in the monument grow on south-facing slopes within lands of the Tohono O'odham Nation or on other government-owned lands. But for the territory gained

by the United States through the Gadsden Purchase in 1853, none would exist in the United States at all.

The northernmost organ pipes (*Stenocereus thurberi*) grow no more than 100 mi. north of the border. A few have survived that far north in the Slate Mountains on the lands of the Tohono O'odham and in the Sand Tank Mountains in what has become the Sonoran Desert National Monument. Ninety percent of American organ pipes are found within about 20 mi. of Mexico, all of them in a pocket of desert virtually free from deep freezes in the winter and moistened by a few thunderstorms in the summer and light rains in the winter. These conditions are critical to the organ pipe's survival. One large and solitary wild individual has established itself on a *bajada* in the Picacho Mountains near Eloy,

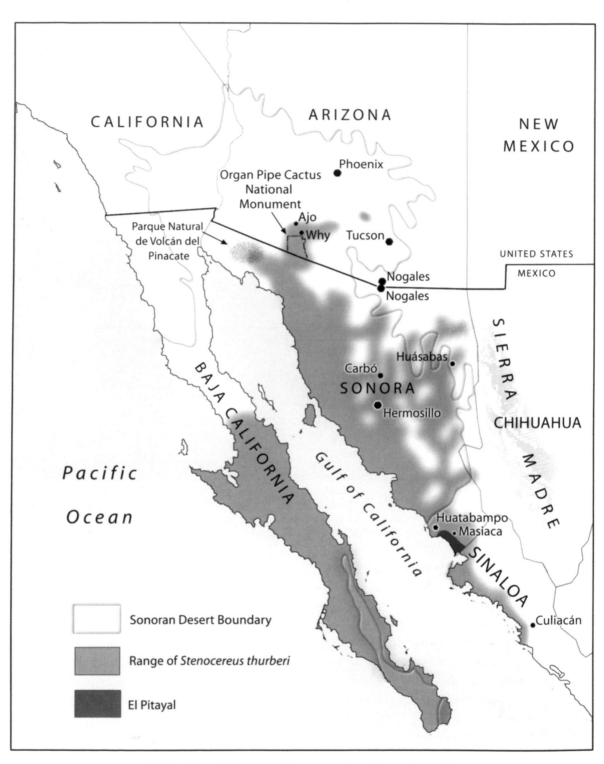

CALIFORNIA

ARIZONA

NEW MEXICO

Phoenix

Organ Pipe Cactus
National
Monument

Ajo
Why
Tucson

Parque Natural
de Volcán del
Pinacate

Nogales
Nogales

UNITED STATES
MEXICO

SIERRA

Huásabas

Carbó

SONORA

Hermosillo

CHIHUAHUA

BAJA CALIFORNIA

Gulf of California

MADRE

Pacific

Ocean

Huatabampo
Masiaca

SINALOA

Culiacán

Sonoran Desert Boundary

Range of *Stenocereus thurberi*

El Pitayal

Distribution of the organ pipe cactus. (Map by Paul Mirocha)

Arizona. Another survives on Desert Peak, an insignificant little mountain northeast of Marana. That plant, a heroic outlier, large, many-branched, and in good health (but damaged by a freeze in 1978), is surely the northeasternmost organ pipe in the United States. The Sand Tank loner is a large, robust plant well concealed in a dense forest of saguaros.

Some researchers refer to these lonesome plants as "advance disjuncts." That is, as organ pipes expand their range northward in fits and starts, these scouts have jumped out well in front of the main force. They carry on in solitude, more than 10 mi. away from their nearest compatriots and 20 mi. from the next closest populations. The fact that they have survived into flourishing adulthood offers the hope that more plants will someday grow in these solitary mountains and maybe even farther north and east.

Organ pipes are called *pitayas* in Sonora and were called that for centuries in Arizona prior to being christened *organ pipes*. The Spanish word *pitaya* is apparently derived from a word of Caribbean origin. Throughout Mexico *pitaya* refers to the fruit of several cacti, primarily members of the genus *Stenocereus*. In Sonora the plants and fruits are referred to as *pitaya*, and elsewhere the plant is referred to as *pitayo*. In northwestern Sonora the fruit and the plant are called *pitaya dulce*, or "sweet pitaya." The pitaya is also an important plant in Sinaloa, where it is called *pitaya marismeña* ("maritime pitaya"). Each year in July and August many poor families from the hills migrate to its coast to gather and sell the fruits.[7]

Six hundred miles southeast of Lukeville, well within the state of Sinaloa, organ pipes become few and show up only sporadically. They disappear for good about 175 mi. south of the Sonora-Sinaloa state line, near the latitude of Culiacán, Sinaloa, the state capital.[8] What causes them to fade out? Organ pipes are desert plants, and too much rain halts their advance farther south in Sinaloa. Annual rainfall near the coast slowly increases south of the Sinaloan border and the progressively richer and more tropical thornscrub apparently crowds out young pitayas. Somewhere south of Culiacán, annual precipitation makes an abrupt leap, reaching in excess of

24 in. annually; with the increased wetness, thornscrub merges into tropical deciduous forest. The organ pipes disappear and a more tropical species, *Stenocereus martinezii* (also called pitayo), a treelike relative found only in Sinaloa and a bit to the south, takes its place. *Stenocereus martinezii* seems to thrive in taller and denser forest. At one time the ranges of these two species might have met and the plants comingled. Organ pipes might even have evolved from these Sinaloan cousins.

Today, however, tracking the original southern limits of the organ pipes has become impossible. Truly colossal acreages in Sinaloa where pitayas once abounded have been cleared of native vegetation and converted to irrigated commercial agriculture. At one point during my search, I drove more than 100 mi. without leaving the leveled fields. Along the highway I tried to locate places where forty years ago I could drive my motor scooter off the pavement into the *monte* (the bush, the natural vegetation), following cattle paths until I found a well-concealed place to pitch my camp. I failed to relocate a single one of the old haunts or any organ pipes. Where the plow has turned the soil, all vestiges of cacti have disappeared along with all other native plant species. So, it is fruitless to wonder just how far south the organ pipe might once have reached. The last one I saw while heading south had made its stand on a small hill too large to level, not worth the effort to clear.

To the east, in the inland portions of southern Sonora, organ pipes also gradually become scarce and then disappear in the more heavily forested portions of the foothills and mountains of the Sierra Madre Occidental. Here, however, the reasons for their disappearance are ecological, not mechanical. With increased elevations, rainfall becomes more abundant. Plants grow taller and thicker with the greater moisture, battling it out with each other for space, so that during the rainy season the whole region resembles a jungle. This seasonally lush forest is too thick and tall for the pitayas' liking, and they become fewer and fewer. Isolated individuals grow on rocky cliffs and on bedrock near canyon bottoms, but in this emerald green forest, which can be so dense that it is impossible to walk through, pitayas cannot get enough

Etcho, Pachycereus pecten-aboriginum, near Teachive, Sonora.

sunlight. Farther up the mountains, usually where large oaks and pines appear, the climate becomes too cold. Yécora, Sonora, in the Sierra Madre at roughly 5000 ft. (1500 m) elevation, can be snowy and freezing in the winter. It is no place for organ pipes.

In the foothills country of southeastern Sonora, the great *etcho* cactus (*Pachycereus pecten-aboriginum*) becomes more common than the pitaya. The etcho is a distant relative of the organ pipe that competes quite well with other plants in foothills thornscrub and tropical deciduous forest.[9] It also becomes the most common tall cactus along Mexican Highway 15 between Guaymas and Ciudad Obregón and in the vicinity of Alamos, Sonora. Etchos form a part of coastal vegetation as far south as Chiapas.

The lushest tropical forest in Sonora grows in the far south, inland near the Sinaloan line. At El Chinal,

Sonora, an isolated village in this forested hill country of the Río Fuerte drainage, the pitaya again becomes noticeably absent. Another, much larger close relative, the *sahuira* (*Stenocereus montanus*) steps in to take its place, for in this region pitayas can survive only on rock outcroppings and on a few rocky, south-facing hillsides. A massive cactus with more uniformly upright branches than the organ pipe, the sahuira is unknown on the coastal plain or in the thornscrub. Why does it suddenly show up here and on the slopes of the Sierra de Alamos? El Chinal is wetter and more tropical than any place on the Sonoran Coast, and the thick tropical deciduous forest that blankets the surrounding hills is inhospitable to pitayas. Except for this jungly area and the hyperarid Gran Desierto, however, pitayas are abundant and flourish in nearly all the remainder of Sonora below 2000 ft. (600 m) elevation.

Sahuira, Stenocereus montanus, near El Chinal, Sonora. The author's nephew, Benton Yetman, stands beneath the cactus.

Organ pipes are columnar cacti, as are saguaros and the very rare (in the United States) *sinita* (*Lophocereus schottii*). Columnar cacti are those whose trunks and branches tend to resemble upright columns and are taller than most humans. (Just what is or is not a columnar cactus is somewhat subjective.) The tall cacti have been a part of the flora of the Sonoran Desert only for the last few million years.[10] The organ pipe is more abundant in northern Sonora and southwestern Arizona now than it was around the end of the last ice age. Organ pipes are relative newcomers to the northern Sonoran Desert: they appeared on the scene only about 3500 years ago in what is now the United States, immigrants from Mexico.[11] The saguaro, more capable of tolerating cold temperatures, arrived far earlier. Its citizenship is better established: saguaros have been around for millennia, having arrived just as the climate began to warm and to dry out, about 10,000 years ago. By then the great continental glaciers were in full retreat and the oceans were rising due to the melting ice.

Sinitas (senitas), Lophocereus (Pachycereus) schottii, near Kino Bay, Sonora.

How can we know these dates? It is thanks to the pack rat (*Neotoma* spp.), which fussily gathers all manner and sizes of materials for its huge nest, then urinates in the whole huge mess. The rats build these jumbles of potpourri inside small caves or rock overhangs, where they are protected from rain. The eons' worth of urine accumulating in the untidy hodgepodges of local plants gradually fossilized and thus preserved the ancient plant parts and pollen grains trapped within. Researchers study samples from the nests (middens), identify the parts and the pollen, and are able to form an accurate idea of what plants were around long ago. Using carbon-14 dating procedures, scientists can determine the age of the middens and what plants were growing in the middens' vicinity at the time. From these studies we know that 10,000 years ago the climate of southwestern Arizona was considerably cooler and moister than now. Oaks and junipers (frost-tolerant species) grew on hillsides that now support only saguaros and palo verdes.[12] The first plant parts from organ pipes appear about 3500 years ago in this fossil record.

If the global climate continues to grow warmer, we can expect organ pipes to migrate into territory where saguaros are now the only columnar cactus. At the same time, saguaros should expand their current range into regions where columnar cacti do not currently grow. Sinitas (or *senitas*, as they are called in Arizona), now confined mostly to a rather small bajada in the southern part of the Organ Pipe Cactus National Monument called Senita Basin, may also expand northward and eastward as well. (Advance disjuncts of sinitas inhabit the Santa Rosa Mountains to the north and east of the monument.) If and when the next ice age comes, or if the climate of the Sonoran Desert continues to become drier as well as hotter (both species are less drought-tolerant than the saguaro), the pitayas' range may instead contract, and they may retreat entirely into Mexico.

Although the organ pipe is uncommon in the United States, it is hardly a rare plant. *Stenocereus*

Fence of *yatos*, *Stenocereus griseus*, Bonaire, Netherlands Antilles.

thurberi is the most common columnar cactus in mainland northwestern Mexico, probably the second or third most common of the more than 100 species of columnar cacti in the world. Before much of its habitat was cleared for agriculture, the organ pipe was probably the world's most abundant columnar cactus. The only exceptions might be the widely cultivated *yato* (*Stenocereus griseus*) of the southwestern Caribbean (see above photo) and the huge and widespread *cardón sahueso* (*Pachycereus pringlei*) of the Sonoran Coast and Baja California (probably the most common now; see photo on page 12) The etcho, or cardón,[13] is also common, growing sporadically from central Sonora along Mexico's western and southern coasts as far southeast as Chiapas. The organ pipe's range is less than half of that of the etcho, but within its range it is far more abundant. Outside of Sonora and Sinaloa, large numbers of organ pipes are to be found in much of the southern half of the Baja California peninsula and in drier portions of the canyon country of southwestern Chihuahua, including the upper Río Mayo and the Barranca del Cobre. The largest populations (and the largest plants), however, are found in Sonora, where the plants prosper by the millions.

The pitaya is certainly the most familiar plant in Sonora. In much of the Sonoran Desert it greatly outnumbers saguaros.[14] Indeed, it might share honors with the saguaro as a symbol of the Sonoran Desert. The densest growth of organ pipes, however, lies to the southeast of the southern boundary of the Sonoran Desert, Arroyo Cocoraque on the coastal plain of the Gulf of California.[15] (Pockets of dense forests grow to the north as well.) From near Huatabampo, Sonora, south and east to the Sinaloa border, the numbers of pitayas seem incalculable. The forest once may have continued well into Sinaloa, but it has long since been cleared for agriculture. In places, more than 175 per acre (430 per ha)—more than half of them large, mature plants—grow intermixed with several species of small tropical trees and a dozen additional species of cactus.* This is El Pitayal

---

* This number is far less than the 3240 individual *sahuesos* per acre (8000 per ha) documented by Ray Turner (Turner et al. 1995) on a small island near Guaymas, Sonora. However, the comparison must be qualified by the fact that the bulk of the sahuesos in that marvelous population are single stalked and many are young plants, while all the *pitayas* are multiple branched and nearly all are mature. Thus, the pitayas require considerably more space per plant than do the sahuesos.

Grove of exceptionally large *sahuesos, Pachycereus pringlei,*
Kino Bay, Sonora.

(vegetation dominated by pitayas), a national treasure of Mexico, an eerily strange, spectacular landscape.

For the most part, unless cattle have trampled the foliage or roadways have been cleared, the vegetation of this well-named thornscrub is so spiny, thorny, and grabby that it is nearly impenetrable. Where trails make passage possible, an amble through the dense growth of pitayas can be compared only with walking through some of the world's great forests. The multitude of angular arms seems to crisscross all available space, creating an exotic pattern of sunlight. The terrain is unvaryingly flat, and the dense, short forest blocks the view in all directions.

On a cloudy day one can easily become disoriented and lost in the seemingly endless expanse of cactus, shrubs, and short trees. The only sounds are the calls and songs of birds, the occasional buzz of insects, and a rustle here and there of a lizard or rodent. In the heat of summer it can become deathly quiet. Cows and goats have created trails randomly. Although the local livestock varieties are by necessity tough, in some places the going is daunting, even for them.

In addition to its transcendent beauty, El Pitayal's organ pipes produce hundreds of tons of valuable fruits each year. Unfortunately for plant fanciers and

El Pitayal, organ pipe cactus forest, Masiaca Indigenous Community, Sonora. Vicente Tajia stands within the grove.

fruit harvesters, the densest forests of all—those occurring near the southern limits of the pitaya's range just north of the Sinaloan border—have vanished. Huge earthmovers eradicated the forest to make way for commercial export agriculture and shrimp farms. Just prior to the bulldozing of the densest part of the forest, I asked a member of the Ejido Agiabampo, where the finest groves were located, what they would do afterward for the fruits and lumber he and his Mayo ancestors had harvested for centuries from the doomed pitayas. He responded with a shrug and added that there would still be plenty on the slopes of some adjacent low-lying hills. Pitayas grow there, but not in impressive numbers. Not in the magical formations of El Pitayal.

In the United States the organ pipe grows mostly on south-facing slopes, hardly ever in low-lying, somewhat flat areas. The plants survive best on hillsides facing south and east. In winter months these locations intercept the earliest morning rays of sunshine and begin to warm, while organ pipes on bajadas (gentle alluvial slopes) or flats below or on slopes that face north or west must wait longer and consequently suffer greater exposure to cold. Organ pipe seeds may germinate in the cooler locations less blessed with morning sun, but the shoots and seedlings stand a greater chance of being killed or maimed by freezing.

Plants on slopes also benefit from the fact that warm air is lighter than cold air and tends to rise. In winter warm air rising from the desert floor coats the hillsides with a blanket of slowly rising warmth, and these gentle currents usually ward off frost. In contrast, the heavier cold air seeps down slopes into drainages and tends to collect in layers at low spots, inhibiting the growth and development of organ pipes there. Anyone who has ridden a motorcycle or bicycle in the desert on a cool morning has experienced the sharp drops in temperature in dips and washes. A large organ pipe cactus flourishes near the Desert Laboratory atop Tumamoc Hill in Tucson, where it was planted many decades ago. The minimum temperatures in winter at the hill's summit are as much as 20°F (12°C) warmer than in the Santa Cruz River terrace at its base,[16] where the cactus could never have survived.

Finally, the rock substrate the organ pipes prefer at their northern limits absorbs and retains heat. When the sun goes down, the rock radiates the stored heat just as heated stones wrapped in blankets warm a cold bed, raising the temperature just a few degrees higher than in places where soils are better developed but have no convoluted rock masses to retain the heat.

A close check of most organ pipes in the Organ Pipe Cactus National Monument reveals a history of on-going trauma. Very few of the branches are continuously smooth from the base to the tip. When the branches show bulges, branching, constrictions, or dead crowns, they have been harmed one way or another, usually by cold temperatures. Organ pipes evolved from tropical cacti and do not tolerate frost well, so their northward march into Arizona has not been easy. At Organ Pipe Cactus National Monument the average winter brings seventeen frosts,[17] but years may pass without a hard freeze. Sooner or later, however, a cold snap will zap the great cacti as temperatures drop into the twenties and remain below freezing for twelve hours or so. Nearly every mature plant in Arizona has experienced run-ins with freezing and bears the scars, if not of frostbite, then at least of tissue damage at the growing tip.

As is the case with all cacti, organ pipes are mostly water stored in greatly expandable cells. Though cooler temperatures retard the growth activity of cacti, they remain at least marginally active photosynthetically in winter; that is, they retain their green color, unlike deciduous trees that drop their leaves and alter their biochemical activity during winter. Only a few primitive cacti have leaves.[18] The others carry on photosynthesis in the green tissues of their trunks and branches; hence, it is vital that that tissue not be destroyed. The freezing of meristematic tissue (the new growth at the tips of branches) apparently kills or stunts some or all of the growth of the organ pipe branches and restricts the following year's growth cycle. The constrictions, branching, or swellings are demonstrations of their constant, nearly annual battle with cold. So

each organ pipe cactus is a historic thermometric record of sorts. Where it grew, sustained temperatures well below freezing cannot have occurred.

But organ pipes also crave heat—lots of it and of many months' duration. Nearly everywhere that the plants grow the maximum temperature exceeds 100°F (38°C). The few exceptions may be indicative of individual plants that possess some genetic resistance to cold: a few can be found in eastern Sonora at 3700-ft. (1100-m) elevations, in the foothills of Mexico's Sierra Madre interspersed incongruously with oaks and palms and pines not far above, and they reach at least 4000 ft. (1250 m) elevations in Baja California's Sierra de la Laguna. At these elevations, temperatures seldom reach 100°F (38°C). In general, though, organ pipes like it hot.

Even so, their heat tolerance has limits. The scorching deserts of extreme northwestern Sonora and south-western Arizona are too hot and probably too dry for organ pipes (and nearly any other cactus). Still, some of them thrive in the burning sands and volcanic hills on the eastern side of the Pinacate Volcanic Range and a few persist in the Cabeza Prieta National Wildlife Refuge, enduring temperatures in excess of 122°F (50°C) and droughts so severe that more than a year may pass without rainfall. In these torridly hot places, organ pipes survive only near *arroyos* (dry washes) or in rocky places where occasional runoff from rainstorms collects and provides a rare sustained drink to the plants' roots and permits the branches to swell with stored water. Generations of selection have enabled these durable plants to tough it out in the brutal heat: on a lava flow in the Pinacate one has been measured at nearly 24 ft. (7.2 m) in height.[19]

Survival of such large plants in ovenlike environments requires highly specialized adaptations. Terrestrial cacti are highly efficient water harvesters, and organ pipes are no exception. Studies with barrel cacti revealed that within twelve hours of a rain, water will penetrate the entire plant. Within a few days it may become fully hydrated, that is, it will have absorbed its maximum possible water, swelling almost to the bursting point. Because most cacti roots lie close to the surface, they

Knobby organ pipe, *Stenocereus thurberi*, Organ Pipe Cactus National Monument.
Such knobs often portray a record of frosts and freezing.

can intercept even small amounts of rain—as little as 0.25 in. (6.25 mm)—and transport it to their stems and branches.[20] This quick absorption is made possible by water roots, root projections that spring rapidly into action when they are dampened, and to the quick rejuvenation of roots that have dried and languished in the prolonged absence of moisture. Along with the quick work of once-dormant roots, the ribs of columnar cacti enable the plants to expand and contract, accordion-like, as they lose or gain water. With abundant rain, they swell until they seem fat and sassy.

In addition to being consummate opportunists in taking in water, cacti have a thick cuticle or waxy outer layer that helps them drastically curtail water loss. Equally important for conserving water, cacti incor-

porate Crassulacean acid metabolism (CAM), cellular machinery for producing the sugars necessary for growth and sustenance.[21] Using CAM, cacti work at night when temperatures are cooler to perform functions that non-CAM plants carry on during the day, thus saving huge amounts of precious water. Cacti share CAM with a few other families of succulent plants. Without CAM, cacti could not survive in hot deserts.

Organ pipes that grow in more moist conditions with less heat extremes have lower drought tolerance. In El Pitayal forest, thousands of large mature plants died in the continuing drought that began in the mid-1990s and continued into the twenty-first century. Some were already old and died a few years prematurely. Others died while comparatively young as a result of a drought

Organ pipe on volcanic rock, Himalaya, Sea of Cortés, Sonora.

unmatched since the great Medieval Drought, which occurred from roughly 1000 to 1300 CE.

Organ pipes tolerate soils ranging from solid rock to the finest silt. They flourish on rocky volcanic slopes overlooking Topolobampo Bay on the Gulf of California's Sinaloan coast. They seem to prosper equally well in granite and calcareous (limestone) soils. Occasionally they will grow as solitary individuals on nearly sheer rock faces or otherwise sterile rock outcrops. Organ pipes survive on thin, young soils in steamy tropical deciduous forests near Alamos, Sonora, to the edges of the extremely dry and sandy Gran Desierto, which, with contiguous deserts, is the driest area in North America. Millions grow in deep clay soils adjacent to the Sea of Cortés in the southern Sonoran lowlands, where they form (or used to form) dense forests. Organ pipes grow in abundance on volcanic and granitic substrate on Tiburón Island off the Sonoran Coast. A few survive on the volcanic rock and sand of the much smaller and drier San Esteban Island, where they are, for the most part, restricted to the northwestern side.[22] Some manage to eke out a living near Quitobaquito Spring in Organ Pipe Cactus National Monument in saline soils with a pH of 10.[23]

In Baja California, organ pipes occupy equally varied habitats, from granite slopes south of Cataviñá at the midpoint of the peninsula south to Cabo San Lucas at the tip. They occupy nearly all habitats of Baja California Sur, except for the Vizcaíno Desert, where it is too dry and summer rains are absent, and the Sierra de la Laguna above roughly 4300 ft. (1300-m) elevation. Unlike the giant cardón sahueso, however, only in a few places do they occupy the same habitat as the sensationally odd boojum trees (*Fouquieria columnaris*). Most organ pipes are to be found in the southern half of the peninsula while the boojums are concentrated in the northern half. Organ pipes apparently require summer rains, which are usually absent or minimal in the northern portions of Baja California where boojums grow and produce such a strange landscape.

How Organ Pipes Live and Grow

THE APPEARANCE of *Stenocereus thurberi*, its profile or habit—or zen, as a friend of mine calls a plant's physiognomy—varies considerably over its range. In areas where frosts are likely to occur, as in Organ Pipe Cactus National Monument, in the drier portions of Sonora that receive less than 4 in. (100 mm) of rainfall, and in central Baja California, it grows multi-stemmed, branching from the ground to somewhat over 15 ft. (4.5 m) tall, occasionally more. Under these conditions, plants are more like shrubs than trees. In the coastal thornscrub[24] of central and southern Sonora and in the southern portion of Baja California, the organ pipe becomes treelike and may reach 35 ft. (10 m) in height. In even wetter foothills thornscrub and tropical deciduous forest, the organ pipe is less common but often grows to a very large size, as tall as 40 ft. (13 m), some individuals developing thick trunks supporting hundreds of branches. On the southwestern slopes of the Sierra San Francisco in central Baja California, the plants are stunted and often covered with lichens and ballmosses (*Tillandsia* sp.). But for most of the year the days are warm to hot, ideal for organ pipes. During winter months there, the hills intercept banks of fog that roll in from the Pacific Ocean, 60 mi. (100 km) away, saturating the atmosphere and

Vicente Tajia stands next to an unusually large organ pipe, southern Sonora.

producing ideal conditions for a variety of epiphytic plants. The subspecies *S. thurberi littoralis* found along the extreme southern Pacific Coast of Baja California might be called the bonsai organ pipe, for it seldom grows taller than 3 ft. (1 m).

Larger organ pipes, especially those growing in the uplands of southern Sonora where frosts are rare, sometimes possess an unmistakable trunk rising up to nearly 3 ft. (0.9 m) above the ground. In general, though, the arms of pitayas branch closer to the ground than do those of other tall cacti that may share their habitat—the etcho, saguaro, sahueso, and sahuira, all of which invariably have a discernible trunk. The branches of the pitaya also tend to be thinner and diverge from the vertical axis at a greater angle than those of etcho and sahuira, whose branches tend to emerge horizontally from the trunk for a short distance and then grow upward parallel or at an acute angle to the main axis. At times, especially when they are growing in large numbers, the arms of the organ pipe grow every which way, even downward.

Organ pipe buds.

The tallest columnar cacti approach 70 ft. (21 m) in height, whereas the tallest organ pipes are barely half that. The average height of organ pipes in the great El Pitayal forest is only about 13 ft. (4 m), but some plants there are much taller.[25] The tallest I have seen is a giant with more than 100 branches near Los Tanques, Sonora: it reaches over 35 ft. (10.5 m) in height. I have reliable reports of individuals 40 ft. (12 m) tall.

Because organ pipes often grow in the company of other columnar cacti, the differences among the species can be confusing. One way to distinguish among them is to count the number of ribs on each arm. This number tends to be more or less constant within a species. Organ pipes usually have more ribs (twelve to nineteen) than the other species with which they are associated, except for the saguaro (twelve to thirty), and these more numerous ribs afford a smoother appearance to the branches from a distance than is the case with other columnar cacti in the region: eleven to fifteen for the sahueso, seven or eight for the sahuira, and ten or eleven for the etcho.

Another distinguishing feature of the organ pipe is its yellowish green color. Plants often become a lighter green—nearly yellow—during the long and hot droughts of spring and early summer but usually take on a more distinct green with the arrival of the rains. Other columnar cacti that turn yellow are usually dying. In death the pitaya turns first pale yellow, then whitish. New organ pipe branches tend to be a bright yellowish green. The newly erupted buds are usually brownish pink but often show a smooth reddish or purplish tint as well, compared with the glossy green of saguaros, felty brown of sahuesos, and bristly yellow of etchos. The fruits of organ pipes sometimes turn more reddish just prior to ripening.

The organ pipe's areoles (the raised wartlike structures on the branches from which spines emerge) are 0.4–1.2 in. (1–3 cm) apart, often with a noticeable notch between them. Etchos, saguaros, sahuesos, and sahuiras do not have this notch. On organ pipes the areoles near the tips of the branches are usually covered with a brown to black resin (glandular or areolar trichomes).[26] Only the organ pipe and its close relatives, which live in other parts of Mexico, have these dark, gummy spots.

The number and arrangement of spines on the areoles is another useful key to distinguishing one columnar cactus from another (though it is difficult to remember

Organ pipe branch tip. Note the gummy areolar trichomes and the notch between the areoles.

and tedious to check out). In the organ pipe, spines number as follows: radial (i.e., around the edge of the areole) seven to nine, about 0.4 in. (1 cm) long; central one to three, the bottom one 0.8–2.0 in. (2–5 cm) long. New spines are reddish to dark brown to black, aging to gray, compared with white aging to grayish white on the other species found in the same parts of the Sonoran Desert (see photo above and on pp. 32 and 34).

Perhaps the most telling difference among the various species is that organ pipe branches are thinner, seldom more than 6 in. (15 cm) in diameter, than all except for those of the sinita, which have far fewer ribs. Branches of adult plants of all the other columnar species are much thicker.

Rates of growth vary widely throughout the life and range of *S. thurberi*. The plant begins as a tiny, barely visible, nondescript shoot of two leaves. Only after a few months do tiny spines appear, and even then it is

not easily identifiable as a cactus. For the first few years the young plant lengthens and widens into a distinct small column but remains tiny. The column increases in height and diameter until at an undefined time, but usually not before it is nearly thirty years old, it puts out branches. The first branches often grow parallel to the ground for a bit. Once their way up is unobstructed, however, they often grow straight as organ pipes—that is, until their upward growth is interrupted by freezing, injury, or competition for light from other plants. When this happens, a new branch may emerge at an angle or offset from the old injury, but the new growth, too, will usually then attempt to grow straight upward. Some plants appear cantilevered, but their arms invariably reach upward unless something interferes. Where forests of organ pipes grow in southern Sonora, the arms may grow every which way, but in the end they head upward. Saguaros, often companion columnar cacti of the organ

Organ pipe seedlings at three months, Sirebampo, Sonora. These were planted in a horizontally split, plastic 2-liter soda pop bottle.

pipes,* nearly always have straight trunks from which the first branches emerge at about 6.5 ft. (2 m) above the ground, and they develop far fewer arms. Organ pipes, especially in their drier environments, tend to branch right at or near the ground.

Hard data on ages of organ pipes in Mexico are scarce,[27] but natives assure me that many large lowland plants in southern Sonora are more than 100 years old.[28] Some individuals may be far older. A living fence of pitayas near Masiaca, Sonora, dates from the 1940s. The plants are only medium sized, 17–20 ft. (5–6 m) tall. Under normal circumstances natives regard plants 12–16 in.

(30–40 cm) tall as six to eight years old and a 3-ft. (1-m) plant about fifteen years old. In contrast, at Organ Pipe Cactus National Monument a 3-ft. (1-m) organ pipe is around twenty years old (as opposed to fifty-three years for a saguaro of the same height), and average annual growth for a juvenile plant is about 3 in. (7 cm). Studies by Enriquena Bustamante, a Mexican scientist, showed average growth rates of 0.012 in. (0.03 cm) per day in Mexico near Organ Pipe Cactus National Monument and 0.048 in. (0.12 cm) per day in El Pitayal.[29] In other words, the southern plants grow four times as fast as the northern ones, averaging about 17 in. (42.5 cm) a year in El Pitayal and about 4 in. (10 cm) a year at the monument. After the plants reach a height of around 6.5 ft. (2 m), growth may be more rapid.[30] During wet years in the south, 1 ft. (0.3 m) or more of growth is common, but only some branches show readily visible growth and other branches show no growth at all. Thus,

* The southernmost population of saguaros is found on steep basaltic slopes of Mesa Masiaca in southern Sonora. South of that robust group of plants, tens of millions of organ pipes are to be found, but nary a saguaro. Mayos are familiar with saguaro fruits but consider them inferior to those of the *pitaya*.

growth is not linear, and at present it is impossible to determine the age of an organ pipe by measuring just one branch.

In a study plot established in 2001 at the Mayo village of Sirebampo in extreme southern Sonora, I measured one-year's growth of 15 in. (24 cm) on two plants that had been roughly 3.3 ft. (1 m) tall. The average annual growth of transplanted juveniles in the plot was about 12 in. (30 cm) in height in 2002, a dry summer. In the somewhat wetter summer of 2004 they grew slightly faster. In the wet spring of 2005, some grew more than 12 in. (30 cm). On the other hand, planted cuttings (lengths of branch stuck into the ground) were far slower to grow. Roughly one-half of them sprouted new branches, but none of these grew more than 3 in. (8 cm) a year, and the cut stems did not grow at all.[31] It was as if the cuttings, harvested from branches of older plants, were in no hurry to repeat the growth spurts of their youth.

Branching from a single young stalk does not usually occur in El Pitayal until the plants are around 6.5 ft. (2 m) in height, though earlier branching is not uncommon. At Organ Pipe Cactus National Monument plants 6.5–8.3 ft. (2.0–2.5 m) tall have four to ten arms.[32] Plants begin to flower when they are about 6.5 ft (2 m).[33]

At exactly which time of year organ pipes will grow varies according to their environment. In Organ Pipe Cactus National Monument they grow primarily in

Orchard of *pitayas*, Sirebampo, Sonora. The plants pictured were all transplanted as small juveniles.

the summer, though growth may be from water stored during winter rains.[34] Preliminary growth data from El Pitayal suggested that pitayas there grow throughout the year, but their most rapid growth occurs in response to *las aguas*, the Sonoran term for summer rains, primarily thunderstorms of July through September, or to hurricanes in the fall. This stands to reason, because the winter rains are less reliable in southern Sonora than in southwestern Arizona, and freezes are nearly unknown. In general, the most rapid plant growth there, especially that of the pitayas, occurs during the hot months.

In the Sonoran Desert, most rain falls as a result of summer thunderstorms in July and August, but the percentage of annual rainfall derived from las aguas varies from location to location. In general, the proportion of annual rainfall from summer rains decreases from the southeast to the northwest. In southern Sonora, which lies outside the Sonoran Desert, on average more than 70 percent of annual rainfall originates in the summer storms. These derive from moist air from the Gulf of Mexico, the warm Pacific, and the Gulf of California. *Equipatas* (the Sonoran term for winter rains) are part of cyclonic storms originating in the Gulf of Alaska. El Pitayal is too far south for equipatas to be reliable. At Organ Pipe Cactus National Monument, however, nearly half of the annual rainfall is derived from these winter rains.[35] The variation of summer-winter ratios is substantial, especially in the south. When the usually reliable fall and winter storms follow a dry summer, the percentage of rainfall constituted by las aguas occasionally decreases from near 80 percent to below 50 percent.

In southern Sonora pitayas seem to rejoice in the arrival of las aguas. Their growth response can be dramatic. A few weeks after a good summer soaking, new brilliant green growth on the pitayas is shiny enough to reflect sunlight. Plants send out new branches that first appear as swellings, each about the size of a ping-pong ball. Even stumps of felled plants will not be denied and often sprout these new arms, sometimes several from one stump. In summer on many plants, especially younger ones, the spines emerging from the apex take

Clouds from a lingering *equipata* (winter storm), Organ Pipe Cactus National Monument.
The tall cactus is a saguaro, *Carnegiea gigantea*.

on a distinctly reddish hue. These appear in clusters as they emerge from the growth tip, and after ample rains this small forest of scarlet spines becomes so dense and pronounced that one can easily mistake the mass for a red flower (as I have) or for some new species of cactus. With age and in dry spells the scarlet color of the terminal spines fades, and they assume the common dark or gray hue.

While new growth on existing plants is evident, El Pitayal is notably lacking in young plants. I have been puzzled and troubled by this lack of recruitment since some Mayo friends and I noticed it in the early 1990s. I began doing fieldwork in the region in 1992, and in 1993 I obtained permission to live in a village within the Masiaca Indigenous Community. Several Mayos were kind enough to stroll with me through El Pitayal many dozens of times and teach me about the plants there. We noticed that, while the organ pipe forest of El Pitayal

is of astonishing density, it is composed almost entirely of large, mature plants. Even in the densest part of the forest, plants less than 3 ft. (1 m) tall are not common. Plants smaller than 1 ft. (30 cm) are very scarce. My Mayo colleagues and I have explored many hectares of prime organ pipe habitat scanning the forest floor for juveniles, sometimes on our hands and knees, usually finding only a few, certainly not enough to match the rate of death in old plants. During one walk of more than 3 km through El Pitayal, three of us encountered only a dozen small pitayas. My friends frequently muttered "cáhita," which means "there is nothing" in the Mayo language.

No explanation for this scarcity of young plants seems sufficient. According to conventional wisdom, the appearance of a new generation of pitayas is hampered by high stocking rates of livestock and by sustained droughts. It is true that cows tend to trample the young plants and remove the vegetative cover that seems to protect them from predation by ants and from dehydration and sunburn. Goats and sheep nibble seedlings, often pulling the tender young things up by the roots. Increasing grazing pressure in the last four decades and a sustained drought in the last decade have, according to this conventional view, suppressed the appearance of a generation of younger plants that would carry on when the

Juvenile organ pipe cacti growing in the open near the Sea of Cortés, Masiaca Indigenous Community. The area is grazed, but water sources are more than a kilometer away, so grazing is not heavy.

older ones succumb to the vicissitudes of old age. To add to ecological concerns, it appears that recruitment of replacement plants may occur only in those rare years when timely and abundant rains occur during and slightly after the fruiting season, when conditions will permit the germination of hosts of seedlings, sufficient in numbers to survive attacks of herbivores, both insects and mammals.[36]

The link between recruitment failure, livestock grazing, and rainfall is puzzlingly inaccurate, however. My colleagues and I worked with local people to establish two large ecological reserves within El Pitayal that have been closed to livestock since 1999. We can find no sign of young pitayas. We are mystified by the fact that within these fenced exclosures that abound in mature plants, almost no new plants are to be found, while in an area not far away from the Mayo village of Sirebampo, numerous small plants of varying sizes grow where goats and cattle have subjected the land to catastrophic overgrazing. We sampled a few dozen sites throughout El Pitayal and found only a handful where young pitayas abound. In most places they are nearly or entirely absent. Grazing seems to play no role whatsoever in the relative presence or absence of the young plants. Yet, the great forest of pitayas proves that at least at one time recruit-

ment was wildly successful over a huge area. Whatever factors produced the right conditions many decades ago for that host of new plants are lacking now.

Many Mayos of the Masaica Indigenous Community are also aware of the dearth of young pitayas and are as perplexed as I am by the phenomenon. In 2000 we decided to establish an experimental pitaya orchard in the village of Sirebampo. Since then *comuneros* (members of the indigenous community) have planted orchards in two other villages. In 2004 families in Sirebampo began planting pitaya seeds in household nurseries. Some of these will be transplanted into El Pitayal, so that when the old ones die new ones will be there to take their place. The willingness of Mayos to undertake a reforestation project suggests the intriguing possibility that their ancestors may have planted El Pitayal and are responsible for the great forest (see photo on p. 22).

After many hours of tramping through the monte, my Mayo colleagues and I have concluded that young pitayas usually, but by no means always, require a nurse plant for survival. Most of them germinate and mature for their first few years in shade beneath large shrubs and small trees, where they benefit from richer soils, persistent moisture after rains, protection from extreme temperatures, and slight protection from trampling by livestock. In coastal thornscrub, the most common nurse trees are *palo brea* (also called Sonoran palo verde, *Parkinsonia praecox*); mesquite (*Prosopis glandulosa*); *guayacán* (*Guaiacum coulteri*), a relative of creosote bush; *ocotillo macho* (*Fouquieria macdougalii*), the tree ocotillo; and *jícamuchi* (*Caesalpinia palmeri*), a leguminous shrub or small tree. In those few areas where young pitayas abound, it is not unusual to find ten or

Nurse plant *palo brea*, *Parkinsonia praecox*, Sirebampo, with eleven young organ pipe plants. The smaller cacti are *Mammillaria* sp. The area is intensively grazed by goats and cattle.

more young plants surviving rather well beneath the protective canopy of the nurse plant. Even adult plants seem to grow best when they are afforded some shading and wind protection by adjacent plants, even though they may be organ pipes as well.

In some areas, however, especially within about 1 km of the coast of the Gulf of California, some small pitayas seem to defy the imperative of nurse-plant protection. In that peculiar habitat, they flourish as solitary individuals exposed to full sun in the complete absence of nurse plants. The higher humidity along the coast creates a haze that may shield them from the harshest rays of the sun. In this habitat, however, average adult size is smaller than the average size of the many-branched giants of El Pitayal. The price the unsheltered pitayas pay for their independence may include diminutive size at maturity. Apart from these hardy individuals, most pitayas are susceptible to sunburn. When the monte is bulldozed,

the operators often leave organ pipes standing. These stranded plants usually die in a couple of years, perhaps from sunburn or exposure.

Native peoples who live in pitaya country keep a careful eye on the annual flowering and fruiting cycle of the pitayas, which varies over the pitaya's range. Some plants begin to flower as early as late May, and scattered individual plants continue flowering into November. A strong majority of plants, however, flowers in June and July in the south, perhaps a month earlier in the north, well after the flowering of other columnar cacti that share the organ pipe's habitat. This timing means the organ pipe flowers will not have to share pollinators' efforts with other large cacti, the etchos, sahuesos, and saguaros. The pollinators can concentrate on just the organ pipes.

The buds of organ pipes are smooth, greenish red to greenish pink. The flowers are large, usually about 3 in. (7.5 cm) across, a soft white, the petals often tipped pinkish or lavender. They are gaudy, typical of North American columnar cacti, offering a host of stamens capped with cream-colored anthers, through which pollinators must pass to get at the sweet, rich nectar (see photo on p. 28). Their large size works to their advantage, for the flowers open at night, often soon after sundown, and may remain open well into the following day, even as late as the afternoon if the day is cloudy. The ample nectar chamber produces enough sweet nectar to attract pollinators repeatedly throughout the night.

Although branches may be covered with a dozen or so buds, only a couple of flowers open at any one time. The buds and flowers of plants sprout from the wartlike areoles on the ridge of the ribs along the upper parts of the branches. In the central and southern parts of organ pipe's range, this is usually within 6 ft. (2 m) of the branch tips and still well out of the easy reach of most human collectors. Plants tend to be shorter in the north, and the fruits are more easily accessible to collectors, a point not lost on aboriginal collectors.

Studies near Kino Bay found that the average plant produces about 100 flowers annually, and of these an average of 24 mature into fruits that produce an average of about 350 seeds each, or 8400 per plant.[37] Individual plants in southern Sonora produce many more flowers and up to 90 fruits, with 50 being about average.[38] The number of seeds per fruit varies widely. In the south, fruits that ripen early in the season tend to have fewer seeds than those that ripen later (about 600 versus nearly 2000).[39] Successful flower pollination tends to be lower in organ pipes than in other species. In one study area, less than 30 percent of flowers developed fully into fruits, the lowest percentage among the large columnar cacti of the Sonoran Desert.[40]

Organ pipe fruits ripen later in the year than those of the etcho in southern Sonora and of the sahueso on the central Gulf Coast. They fruit much earlier in the northern part of their range and in Baja California, often in late June, than they do in the southern part. The reason for the north-south discrepancy in fruiting season remains a bit of a mystery and runs counter to what we might imagine. Even in the south disjunct patches of organ pipes mature a month earlier than pitayas only a few miles away. For example, the small village of El Tábelo, some 12.5 mi. (20 km) north of Alamos, Sonora, is noted for the early ripening of its pitayas. In a small area in Seri country pitayas produce two crops of fruits, one in the summer and another in the fall.[41] In all areas, however, the last fruits of saguaros tend to overlap with the earliest organ pipe fruits.

It may be that organ pipe seeds in southern plants require more moist conditions for germination than those of either of the other giants, etchos and saguaros. Maturing at the height of the rainy season rather than prior to it (as is the case with sahuesos) or at the beginning (as with saguaros) affects the probability of germination and places the pitayas well out of competition with the others for the attention of fruit foragers. A wide variety of creatures feast on the fruits—birds, especially doves and Gila woodpeckers and, in the south, white-fronted parrots, and mammals, primarily bats, coyotes, and foxes, which consume and distribute the seed in their feces. Fruits ripen as late as October in El Pitayal. Among Sonoran columnar cacti only fruits of the *pitaya agria* (*S. gummosus*) of the central Gulf Coast ripen so late in the year. These sprawling cacti are more typical of Baja California, where equipatas are more reliable than las aguas. Their fruits are larger than those of *S. thurberi* and are usually considered to be superior to the latter by those who have consumed both.

The extended fruiting season of southern organ pipes leaves the plants with ripe fruits well into the time of the hurricanes. In Sonora these storms strike the region several times each decade and are called *cordonazo de San Francisco* (St. Francis's whip), since they tend to arrive around St. Francis's Day, October 4. Hurricanes strike Baja California more often than they do Sonora, and they can be monster storms that produce prodigious amounts of rain in a short time. Three of them lashed El Pitayal in the 1990s, and each dumped more than 1 ft. (30 cm) of rain in little more than a day on parts of the southern coast. The monte explodes with growth following these huge storms, and pitayas find

Pitaya with buds and developing fruits, Coteco, Sonora. Note the arrangement on the branches. Saguaro fruits tend to be clustered near the apex of the branches.

Organ pipe flower, Teachive, Sonora.

ideal conditions for rapid growth and seed germination. The cordonazos may be related to the plants' survival. I have sometimes worried that the powerful winds accompanying the hurricanes would topple some of the great plants, but my Mayo friends assure me this is not so, and my inspections following the cordonazos have revealed no significant losses.

In the great Pitayal many organ pipe plants bear few fruits and some none at all. This may be a result of the simultaneous pollination requirements of many millions of flowers. Organ pipes are pollinated by bats and hummingbirds,[42] plus other less charismatic foragers, including white-winged doves, flying insects such as bees, and even ants. In the vicinity of Kino Bay, in central Sonora, bats account for only one-third of pollination, while hummingbirds and honeybees account for the other two-thirds.[43] Pitaya numbers along the southern coast may be so vast that during the height of the pitaya flowering season the supply of pollinators is insufficient to attend to the needs of all the flowers.

Fruit eaters are responsible for propagation of most of the plants. They carry the seeds away and excrete them in a fertile medium. In the Pinacate Volcanic Range just south of the border separating southwestern Arizona from northwestern Sonora, bats have laid out a clearly visible trail of organ pipes leading to and from their nesting sites. For many decades, perhaps centuries, bats have eaten the pitaya fruits and defecated the seeds along the way to and from their roosts.[44] The cacti fan out in the direction of their outward flight, thus mapping the direction of their flights and pointing the direction of the food source.

While digestion of the seeds may assist in the rate of seed germination, it does not seem to play a critical role.[45] However, the clear trail left by foraging bats seems to establish that ingestion by herbivores affects distribution and dispersion of the plants. I often wonder how the solitary organ pipes in the Picacho Mountains, Sand Tanks, Slate Mountains, and on Desert Peak came to grow there. Could a maverick bat have pooped a seed onto a fertile spot with just the right temperature and exposure to the sun to permit it to survive? Bats are

known to fly at least 50 mi. (80 km) from their roosts, a distance that brings the isolated locations well into their range.[46] Or could a human have camped nearby after having eaten organ pipe fruits in the Santa Rosa Mountains to the southwest? Could a pitaya have turned rotten in the basket of some human carrier and been discarded right at that spot? Or, could an ancient Johnny Organpipeseed have chosen that spot in which to plant a seed, supposing that a nice organ pipe would enhance the landscape or some day provide free food?

Even more intriguing is a solitary pitaya that is probably the most venerated plant in all of northwestern Mexico, perhaps the entire republic. The 10-ft.-tall plant projects in a most unlikely fashion from ancient rockwork of an exterior church wall in the old mining town of Aduana, Sonora, near Alamos. It probably was deposited in the crevice by a fruit-eating bat or bird that defecated while on the wing. Local legendry places its age at more than 250 years. As the story goes, the cactus sprouted from the southern wall of the church roughly 15 ft. above the ground shortly after the nave was completed in 1730. An apparition, surely that of the Virgin Mary according to the faithful, supposedly appears from time to time between the branches of the cactus. Pilgrims from all over Mexico pay respects to the plant, especially during the November 20–21 festival of the Virgin of Balderrana, when many thousands of the faithful arrive on foot, donkey, horse, bicycle, or motor vehicle to pay homage to the cactus. Hundreds of pilgrims interrupt their partying to lay down blankets and conduct a vigil beneath the pitaya, spending a night or two waiting patiently, hoping for a vision of the Virgin. She has not appeared in recent years. Many of the faithful, still hopeful, leave votive candles behind, so numerous that a veritable river of wax from the thousands of candles flows down the walls and the patio. The residents of the tiny village must clean up the thick strata of paraffin. In the mid-1990s the wax caught fire, singeing the bottom half of the famed pitaya and causing great concern that the plant would die. By the end of the millennium, however, new growth appeared, and the bright green of fresh pitaya showed

Organ pipe growing from church wall, Aduana, Sonora. This plant is the most revered in northwestern Mexico. Note the decorations on the branches.

that the plant was far from dead. The Virgin of the Pitaya is not easily routed.

The survival of this pitaya in such an improbable environment appears more marvelous than any vision. How a plant weighing more than 100 lb. manages to obtain moisture and nutrition in such an unforgiving medium and can hold onto its precarious perch for many centuries is a wonder that invokes the miraculous. Were the rock wall to be dissected, however, it would probably reveal crevices and cavities in the rock and mortar where water is stored during heavy rains, providing the plant with an irrigation source. Perhaps the wonder is that more organ pipes do not take advantage of such private niches. Only succulent (water-storing) plants such as cacti could pull off such a stunt. And only the perfect timing of a seed dropping into a moist cavity will produce such a plant.

The Organ Pipe's Close Relatives

THE GENUS *Stenocereus* contains about twenty-three species; some species are disputed as to genus, others as to whether they constitute a legitimate species, and still others remain identified but undescribed.[47] Most of the Mexican species are commonly referred to as *pitayo* (the plant), while the fruits are called *pitayas*.[48] The species range in size from the rare, prostrate, creeping devil (*S. eruca*) of the Magdalena Bay region of Baja California that never grows upright to the equally rare but gigantic *S. chacalapensis* of the Oaxacan coast that reaches 50 ft. (15 m) in height with a trunk resembling that of a thick ponderosa pine. The *xoconochtli* (*S. stellatus*) of Guerrero, Oaxaca, and Puebla has apparently been culti-vated for millennia. A close relative of the xoconochtli, commonly called the *tunillo* (*S. treleasei*), does not appear to grow in the wild at all and may have evolved as a purely domestic species in Oaxaca during the mil-lennia of plant selection carried out by indigenous horticulturalists in south-central Mexico.[49]

The organ pipe is most closely related to two other columnar cacti of the genus, *S. martinezii* and *S. quevedonis*, and to the shrubby semicolumnar *S. beneckei*.[50] The former two plants are far less wide ranging than organ

Stenocereus chacalapensis, Pacific Coast of Oaxaca. These huge plants grow only within a radius of a dozen kilometers or so.

Buds of a *tunillo*, *Stenocereus treleasei*, Oaxaca. Found only in the central valleys of Oaxaca, this cactus appears to grow only under cultivation.

The author examines a *pitire*, *Stenocereus quevedonis*, southern Michoacán. Although many thousands of these plants grow in the vicinity, they appear to be limited to a few hot valleys in southern Michoacán.

pipes. *Stenocereus martinezii* (called *pitayo*) grows in central Sinaloa as scattered, irregularly shaped trees of medium height with well-defined trunks. The northern end of the range of this pitayo fizzles out not far south of where the southernmost organ pipes dwindle. I have never photographed *S. martinezii*, because where it grows has for years been an area infested with drug-related crime, making the probability of my being shot far greater than I would like. *Stenocereus quevedonis* (commonly called *pitire*) is a very tall columnar cactus similar in appearance to the organ pipe but with a distinct trunk and straighter branches. It grows in huge numbers but only in the vicinity of Presa Infiernillo on the Río Balsas in southern Michoacán, Mexico.

As is the case with organ pipes, areoles on *S. martinezii*, *S. quevedonis*, and *S. beneckei* exude a saplike substance

Pitayo de mayo, Stenocereus pruinosus, Oaxaca. Thousands of these
plants grow in intensely managed orchards.

that dries hard and darkens to reddish or brown or even black[51] to form glandular or areolar trichomes.[52] All three columnars usually exhibit a horizontal notch or crease between the areoles. (It may be lacking or spotty on some branches or even entire plants, but is usually present.) Flowers of the three species are so similar that it takes an expert to tell them apart, which also suggests a close evolutionary kinship. The fruits of *S. martinezii* and

S. quevedonis are also edible and are harvested locally. Their habits, however, are readily distinguishable. If, as seems likely, *S. thurberi* evolved along the same kindred branch with the pitayo and the pitire, the organ pipe was the evolutionary winner, for its range and its numbers vastly exceed those of the other two species.

Based on the species' distributions and similarity of other characteristics, it seems likely that the organ pipe

The author beside an orchard of *pitaya de Querétaro, Stenocereus queretaroensis,* Jalisco. The Sayula Valley of southern Jalisco has more than 2500 acres (1000 ha) devoted to raising these cacti for their fruits.

evolved from the pitayo (*S. martinezii*), which requires more rainfall and is less resistant to damage due to cold. It, in turn, along with the pitire, probably evolved from another member of the genus that evolved in southern Mexico, perhaps in the cactus-rich Valley of Tehuacán and environs in the state of Puebla. In that arid valley grow at least seventeen species of columnar cacti in various stages of evolution. From there, pitaya species proliferate in all directions.[53] Nearly every state in Mexico is home to at least one species of *Stenocereus*. Sonora has four, three of which frequent the Sonoran Desert.[54]

Stenocereus is also a notable genus in that all its members yield sweet, edible fruits in impressive numbers. I have tried nearly all of them (some while they were still unripe) and have yet to be disappointed. Some species tend to be wildly prolific fruit producers. In the Netherland Antilles off the coast of Venezuela, the yato (*S. griseus*) has been so widely cultivated for fruit and fences that it is difficult to find authentically wild plants. For millennia indigenous people in Mexico have lopped off limbs from high-yielding plants and stuck them in the ground for later use as fruit producers, so much so that at least six species (including *S. griseus*) have been semidomesticated. This ongoing selection over centuries has resulted in plants that yield many dozens of baseball-sized, succulent fruits.

In the Mexican states of Jalisco, Michoacán, Oaxaca, Puebla, and Sinaloa, farmers plant orchards of the great

Fruit of *pitayo de mayo*, *Stenocereus pruinosus*, Oaxaca.

cacti from cuttings and market the fruits commercially. I once took some Mayo friends on a trip to visit the pitayo orchards near Guadalajara, Jalisco. Farmers there happily pointed out that they can make more money raising cactus fruits than they can raising traditional crops. Each year in May the municipality of Techaluta in the same valley celebrates a pitaya festival, its most important annual event. Town and city markets in the highlands of southern Mexico usually stock fresh pitayas in the hot months. The various species bear fruit at times ranging from May to October, so for six months of the year the fruits are available commercially somewhere in the region. The yato, the most purely tropical of the genus, seems to bear fruit throughout the year.

Organ Pipes in History

ORGAN PIPES IN THE UNITED STATES are ogled at and fussed over, but for the most part the American plants are not highly exploited by native peoples. For millennia the Tohono O'odham of southern Arizona have taken advantage of saguaros for fruits and building materials, but organ pipes in the United States are few and incapable of producing enough fruits to constitute an important role in the O'odham diet. However, the O'odham of Arizona share a long border with Mexico, and organ pipes proliferate exponentially just south of the border. At the Mexican Tohono O'odham settlement of Quitovac, Sonora, only 25 air miles south of the U.S.–Mexico border, Mexican relatives of Arizona O'odham are vigorous gatherers of pitayas.[55] They make the fruits into preserves and syrup, which they have traded historically with the Akimel O'odham (River Pimas) of Arizona's middle Gila River.[56]

For native peoples of Sonora, the pitaya is probably the most important native plant. In Baja California aboriginal peoples depended on it for survival, and rural Mayos and Yaquis can hardly conceive of life without it.[57] One reason for the persistence of their cultures, which extend back for centuries prior to contact with Europeans, is the ubiquity and reliability of the pitaya. In southeastern Sonora it is the most noticeable plant in coastal thornscrub and one of the most important in the foothill thornscrub community. Organ pipes rise in numbers so vast they are difficult to conceive. The plants seem to overwhelm the landscape. In other areas of central and southern Sonora, the pitaya is codominant with scrubby, primarily leguminous trees (mesquites, ironwoods, *jóconas*, and various *mimosas*[58]) and etchos, which coexist well with pitayas.

The earliest Europeans to chronicle what they saw in northwestern New Spain commented on the variety of uses of organ pipe fruits. Baltazar Obregón wrote in a 1584 report to the Council of the Indies that the natives of the Río Sonora "gather great quantities of *tunas* [fruits of prickly pear cacti] and *pitahayas* and dry them inside, then store them with their seeds in large bins to eat when they need it; they make delicious food."[59] Ignaz Pfefferkorn, a Jesuit missionary to Sonora in the mid-eighteenth century scorned many indigenous foods and customs but was quite taken with pitayas:

> The pitahaya bush grows principally on knolls and hills, although it is also found on flat land. As for size, it could well be called a tree, since it sometimes reaches a thickness of more than two feet [0.6 m] and attains a height of ten to twelve or thirteen ells [an ell equals an arm's length, roughly 45 in. (18 cm)]. Frequently it has ten, twelve, and even more branches, each of which is as thick and as long as the main trunk. These branches extend out horizontally from the trunk for about half an ell; then they bend in an elbow and grow up vertically. Both branches and trunk have longitudinal furrows all around like melons. All are a light green color and are covered everywhere with pointed spines, which, however, the tree gradually loses as it ages. On this admirable shrub grows the sweet, pleasant-tasting pitahaya. It does not hang on small stems like other fruits, but clings directly to the trunk and the branches. Like the rest of the tree, it is entirely covered with spines. In fruitful years there are often several hundred on one shrub. They are in size and shape like a duck egg with a thick, tough, green shell, which becomes

light brown when ripe. The meat of the pitahaya is either white or blood red and is full of black, easily chewed seeds like those found in figs. Red pitahayas are the most plentiful in Sonora; white ones are somewhat scarce. Many Indians open this fruit, lay it in the sun for a day to dry up the abundant juice. They then loosen the meat from the shell and press it very hard into a kind of cake, which is called a tamale. . . . The juice of this fruit is cooked into a blood red honey, which in taste and sweetness is as good as sugar honey."[60]

In the southern half of Baja California, where the pitaya is also common, so vital was the fruit to the Californians' survival that rival indigenous groups competing for groves of the cactus battled over pitaya rights.[61] Furthermore, the various growth stages of the pitaya were the basis for the annual calendar of several peoples of Baja California, the new year beginning with the first pitaya fruits in late June or early July.[62] Fr. Miguel del Barco, writing about Baja California in the mid-eighteenth century, observed of the fruits that "those that have a yellow skin, some have white meat inside, others yellow, and still others buff. All of them are excellent fruit, worthy of the table of the greatest monarchs."[63] Another Jesuit missionary fumed about the natives' fondness for the fruits (the Jesuits often frowned upon regular use of wild foods by natives):

> In the immediate vicinity of our camp were many of the tart pitahaya, the only thing that, throughout the Californias, might be termed a luxury. These were coveted by the Indians; no matter what orders were issued by the captains, and, despite all I could say, they would not restrain themselves. Whenever they went out, hatchet in hand, after wood, or sought water or anything else, they invariably strayed away. So irremediable was this evil that it was a strong temptation to wish that the Californians had never acquired this habit.[64]

Among Baja California peoples the ripening of pitaya fruits ushered in a joyful time when they abandoned all other enterprises (including religious duties) to revel in the sweet fruits and the wine they produced from the fruits, celebrating with dancing and general party-making and what the clerics would have viewed as pagan mischief. It must have been a priest's nightmare. The historian Miguel Vanegas related the following story of a hapless Spanish soldier stationed at a mine in Baja California who had "married" a native woman:

Around the month of June his lover's mother showed up at the mine and convinced her daughter to abandon her lover in order to attend the dances and festivities that accompany the pitaya harvest. The young woman needed little convincing and followed her evil mother's suggestion and they sneaked out at night without being noticed. When the soldier missed his woman, he asked permission of his captain to go search for her and bring her back. The captain granted a short leave. The soldier left with a companion but, not finding her, returned. A few days later, overcome with his passion, he set out alone with a California Indian and left the mine far behind until approaching a distant *ranchería* he heard shouting and an uproar. He happened upon an old Indian to whom he told the reason for his quest. The old man advised him to go back to the mine because his life would be in danger where he was. Furious, the soldier threatened the old man, who remained adamant. In his rage the soldier shot him with his harquebus. Hearing the explosion, the natives of the *ranchería* came running and, surrounding the soldier, shot him full of arrows.[65]

The lure of the pitaya festivities apparently transcended anything the Spaniards had to offer. Another Jesuit was astonished to find the appearance of his native charges greatly altered upon their return to the missions after pitaya season. They gorged themselves for weeks with the fruits, producing rapid and substantial weight gain.[66]

Many peoples of the northwestern mainland of Mexico also favored the pitaya fruits that inspired such reckless and wanton disobedience of the clergy among Baja California peoples. The Jesuit Joseph Och, priest of the mis-

sion of San Ignacio in the late 1750s, made some wistful observations about the fruits: "[The Pimas and Ópatas] made an agreeable beverage using . . . the excellent pitaya fruit whose juice is pressed out by hand in astonishing quantities by old women using mortars hollowed out in rocks. This juice is blood red in color, and if it were not squeezed and pressed under such filthy conditions would be found palatable by the finest gentlemen. . . . These [beverages] have now all been forbidden and the making of them is punishable."[67]

Pedro de Castaneda, in a narrative of the Coronado expedition of 1540, observed of people of what was Ópata (Tegüima and Eudeve) country: they "are inveterate sodomites. They drink the juice of the pitaya, a fruit of big thistles which opens like the pomegranate. They become stupefied with this drink."[68] An older Mayo once mentioned to me that pitaya fruits have aphrodisiac powers and it is this belief, apparently common, as well as the knowledge that the fruits could be used to brew a mildly alcoholic wine that may have struck pious indignation and primordial resolve into the hearts of the priests. Jesuits were instructed strictly to forbid the drinking of wine among their native charges.[69] Natives must have been both puzzled and irritated upon learning that among the first acts of the priests representing their conquerors was the prohibition of those activities that were the most important for them and the most fun.

What the early chroniclers seem to have overlooked (or suppressed) was the cultural significance of the pitayas. The various festivals that surrounded wine drinking, whether from saguaros or pitayas, were not simply parties—although they were that. The annual ritual represented a critically important affirmation of themselves as a people, underscored their inextricable relationship with the natural world, and reminded each person of the cosmic cycle of events that included planting and harvesting of foods.

Cactus wine festivals were the most important annual events for the Pimas (O'odham). Wine fermented from saguaro fruits was the basis for the elaborate *wiikita* (*vikita*) festival among the Tohono O'odham, and the reproductive cycle of the cactus was the basis for the

O'odham calendar. Pitayas took on an added significance because the plants were believed to fruit twice. They were a "friendly fruit," because easily accessible branches were bountifully covered with fruits. So highly regarded was the second fruiting season that the O'odham name for the Milky Way translates as "the second harvest of pitahaya."[70]

Ethnographer Ruth Underhill reported on a pitaya wíikita festival in the Sonoran village of Quitovac during the first full moon of August 1931. (The festivals based on saguaro fruits were observed in July.) She reported that villagers from southern Arizona joined the Mexican O'odham in the festival. They gathered pitaya fruits and began the fermentation a day before the festival. If the fermentation was complete earlier than expected, participants believed it was the wíikita itself that caused the fermentation. The ceremony was expected to produce rain.[71]

Syrup from organ pipe fruit (the raw material for the wine) has a delicate flavor with a most agreeable, mildly astringent aftertaste. Well into the twentieth century River Pimas reported that, although organ pipes do not grow in River Pima country, the syrup was highly regarded and was traded from northwestern Mexico up the Colorado River as far north as Parker, Arizona.[72]

Baja Californians ate the pulp of pitaya dulce as a source of water, enabling them to travel far afield into areas lacking water.[73] They could sustain themselves in summer for several days on the water from pitaya dulce alone. This enabled them to exploit native resources in remote areas that, for lack of drinking water, would otherwise have been inaccessible. I have noted the same phenomenon. When, upon the advice of Mayo friends, I ingest large numbers of pitayas during my fieldwork, though it be in the scorching heat of summer, I need to drink far less water than in hot weather without pitayas. Whether this is due to high water content of the fruits or to a chemical that suppresses thirst remains to be discovered. Water sources are few in Baja California, and the natives appear to have suffered greatly in drought years when the pitaya dulce harvest was poor or insignificant. The fruits of the saguaro, so vital for the

Tohono O'odham, are less juicy and are often harvested after the husk has split open and the pulp has partially dehydrated. Saguaro fruits do not appear to serve this thirst-allaying function.

Several reports from early European visitors assert that after consuming large numbers of pitaya fruits, natives would defecate in special places, then scavenge undigested pitaya dulce seeds from the dried feces, thoroughly clean them, and grind them into a meal.[74] Missionaries and early observers referred to such re-collection delicately as "the second harvest." In very dry deserts, where already sparse rains were notoriously unreliable, failure of food resources could endanger native peoples' survival. The practice of gleaning undigested seeds could mean the difference between starvation and survival.

While the practice is well documented for the seeds of the sahueso, which were also separated from the pulp and stored by the Seris, it is doubtful that the seeds of pitaya dulces were so re-collected anywhere outside of Baja California. In the case of the Seris, only the sahueso seeds were used in the second harvest.[75] Pitaya seeds are tiny, far smaller than those of the sahueso, so much so that of the dozens of pitaya consumers I have known, none has collected the seeds of fresh fruits. Fr. Miguel del Barco, writing in the eighteenth century of the pitayas of Baja California, accurately described the seeds as smaller than mustard seeds, meaning that re-collecting them would require a huge investment of labor for relatively little caloric return. Some indigenous people of Sonora still separate the much larger seeds of the etcho from the pulp (prior to ingestion), but no one seems to think it would be worthwhile to save pitaya seeds. So it seems likely that some of the reported chroniclers of the second harvest were observing the results of undigested sahueso seeds, not those of the pitaya. While I believe we can exclude the organ pipe from this unusual aspect of ancient native life in the dry desert of Sonora, Fr. del Barco was adamant that in Baja California pitaya seeds were also the object of the second harvest, and his observations were so meticulously detailed that they must be taken seriously.[76]

Five

Mayos and Organ Pipes

Peoples who use or used the organ pipe to great advantage include Cáhitas, Guarijíos, Hia Ced O'odham, Pimas, Lower Pimas, Seris, Tohono O'odham, Rarámuri (Tarahumara), and the now-extinct Ópatas (Tegüimas and Eudeves). Among the Lower Pimas, especially large plants are found in the thornscrub along the Yaqui River near Ónavas, Sonora. In Mountain Pima country, pitayas are common in the vicinity of Onapa and Guisamopa in the upper Sahuaripa Valley, where they would have been well known to natives.

Pitayas have played an especially important role in the lives of Mayos and Yaquis, both of whom inhabit the southern coastal plain of Sonora. Their languages, grouped under the label Cáhita by linguists, are closely related. The Mayo language contains many terms for *aaqui*—the cactus—and its parts, and the Yaqui language shares at least some of the terminology.

Mayos live in the southernmost portions of Sonora, from the Río Mayo south to the Río Fuerte in Sinaloa. They number about 60,000. A tiny percentage of them speak only the Mayo language, and perhaps one-third are fluent in Mayo and Spanish. The remainder speak only Spanish. About half of the Mayo live in small traditional villages well dispersed throughout the vast monte of the coastal plain and foothills, which also happens to contain the highest densities of pitayas. Nearly every traditional Mayo house in the region incorporates pitaya wood in some form or another. In a few hamlets, the most notable feature is the myriad fences of pitaya ribs that surround the houses. Some of these measure 1000 ft. (300 m) around. This is pitaya country, the center of the organ pipe's intimate relationship with humans.

A great deal of what I have learned about the pitaya was pointed out to me by Mayos, especially Sr. Vicente Tajia of Teachive, a small village in the thornscrub of the Masiaca Indigenous Community of southern Sonora. For Vicente, and for nearly all rural Mayos, the pitaya is the most important native plant. Over the years Vicente has provided me with informal lectures about the pitaya: how to cut a *quiote* (flowering stalk of agave) to make a *bacote* (gathering stick) and fashion a *punta* (point) from *pisi* (a small tree, *Randia thurberi* or *R. obcordata*, Rubiaceae), and how to pierce *huásim* (the ripe fruit) at the base and wiggle it free without inflicting a punitive leak in the fruit's side. He has demonstrated the proper harvesting technique dozens of times, but I never caught on. Vicente also showed me—usually with a pedagogical flourish—a lot about the plants. He has noted which plants have the best fruits, whether the normal *rojo* (red), the less common *zarca* (white), the even less common *amarilla* (yellow), or the very rare *guinda* (purple). Vicente also demonstrated how to excise branches and lop off the green matter for preparing the ribs to construct *chinámim* (pitaya fences) and that fallen branches will take root and grow into large plants. I have also benefited from spending considerable time with residents of the village of Sirebampo in El Pitayal. Several pitaya experts there accompanied me on long jaunts through the organ pipe forest and shared their considerable knowledge of the cactus and its ways.

Because pitayas grow in greatest density in Mayo country and because pitaya terminology is so widespread there, I will describe some of the uses of the cacti and the Cáhita terms.[77] In discussing pitayas with many villagers, I have found the knowledge and terminology to be widely disseminated. Just about every rural Mayo and Yaqui knows a lot about pitayas. When the fruits are ripe, scores of Cáhita people spend numerous hours in the monte, gorging themselves and filling buckets of the fruits to take home or to sell (see photo on p. 43). In the process they have come to develop an impressive body of knowledge about the plants. They have gently corrected me from time to time in some pronouncements I have made about the plants, and I have learned not to draw conclusions about pitayas without checking first with the people who know them best.

Rural Mayos gobble up the sweet, satisfying pulp of the fruits (*aaqui tej'ua*)— usually a little larger than a ping-pong ball—in great quantities in late July, August, and September. The pulp constitutes an important component of the Mayo and Yaqui summer diet and a potentially valuable economic resource. Many people report that they eat more than fifty fruits per day. Mayos say that "one never gets tired of eating them" (*No se enfada uno*). I share this opinion. I've eaten forty in a day and could have eaten more.

Formerly, most people dried the fruits (particularly in inland locations where humidity is lower), but this practice has fallen from popularity in recent years. They also preserved the fruits or made them into wine. That worthy practice of brewing seems to have been abandoned in recent decades, probably corresponding with the proliferation of popular Mexican beers and the heavy promotion of beer as the socially mandatory beverage. Drinking home-fermented wine is popularly associated with Indians, and to be Indian in Mexico is to be socially stigmatized: the term *indio* is disparaging.[78] Many young Indian people seem anxious to escape being labeled *indio* and dissociate themselves as much as possible from traditional non-Mestizo customs. Gathering pitayas, making wine, and marketing the fruits are all carried on, for the most part, by very poor or traditional Indians.

Drying the fruits requires greater effort than is the case for saguaro fruits. Unlike the saguaro, pitaya fruits do not appear to dry within the husks while still attached to the plant (except perhaps at higher elevations and farther inland). This may be due to higher humidity in the pitaya's range and more numerous animal consumers, but it also reflects water content that is higher than that of saguaro fruits and the tendency of the husks of saguaro fruit to split open widely, thus exposing the pulp to the full sun.[79] Fruits of pitayas are also more likely to ferment or become rotten and unusable while still attached to the plant and after harvesting than either those of the saguaro or the sahueso.

During the ripening season, the pitaya groves are abuzz with countless nonhuman fruit eaters—many species of birds (especially white-winged doves, white-fronted parrots, and Gila woodpeckers), bats, and innumerable insects such as ants, bees, wasps, and beetles. *Pitayeros* watch for these creatures and quickly become expert at gauging the readiness of fruits for harvesting. Picking green fruits is foolish, for they are hell to dislodge from the branches and the spines cannot be removed from the skins unless stripped away with a knife while the fruit is held down with something other than fingers. When the fruits are ripe, they pull away from the branches with little effort by the picker, and the spines easily slough off. I have never developed the keen eye for ripeness needed by a pitayero. I sometimes select fruits that are overripe and, more often, those that need another day on the branch. Most pitayeros can see differences I find indistinguishable.

Occasionally native women make and market tamales (*aaqui nójim*) from the fruits. The best tamales are made from *poposáhuim* (nearly ripe but unopened fruits). The women deftly remove the spiny husks and lay globs of fruit on a cloth suspended over a wide-mouthed container. They then squeeze the cloth at both ends to wring out the juice. Children sometimes sneak in and try to drink the juice at this point, but women shoo them away. The women boil the pulp until it thickens, pour it into cornhusks, twist the ends, and allow the *tamal* to cool. The tamales are sweet and tasty but messy to eat.

In scattered locations, people also prepare pitaya seca (dried organ pipe fruit). It is usually made in small batches of a couple of dozen ripe fruits that are boiled in a skillet with a little water. The boiled or blended mixture (*beja buásic*) is strained through a coarse piece of cloth to remove excess *miel* (syrup). The remaining, rather slimy, mass is spread out to dry and covered with a screen to keep out flies and other insects. When properly dried, the pitaya seca is tacky and chewy but not damp. It will remain edible for several months. Older Mayos still use a raised bed called a *tapanco* constructed from slats of dried ribs of the pitaya cactus laid side by side and close together to store the drying fruit and protect it from dogs and pigs. Preparing pitaya seca during the height of las aguas is risky, however, because the high humidity retards drying and encourages molds, which quickly render the product inedible.

In the northern parts of the pitaya's range fruits ripen earlier, usually by early July, than they do farther south. The northeastern Sonoran town of Huásabas on the Río Bavispe is well known for abundant harvests of pitaya fruits. Inhabitants of the town report that the name is an Ópata[80] word meaning, "Where the pitayas first ripen." Humidity is much lower around Huásabas than on the coast, and local residents dry the fruits by laying them out on drying racks in the full sun. Seris who live along

Ripe *pitayas*, Sirebampo, Sonora. María de Jesús Buitimea fans fruit flies away.

Trays of drying *pitaya seca*. Mayos sometimes include mango fruit for
its long fibers.

the coast of the Sea of Cortés in central Sonora once did the same. Rainfall in their country is roughly one-fifth that of El Pitayal, so lower humidity made fruit drying possible.

By late June the earliest fruits ripen in the north, and vendors hawk them at traffic lights in Hermosillo (those from the vicinity of Carbó and Rayón are said to be the sweetest). In southern Sonora, however, serious collecting seldom begins prior to late July or even early August, when prodigious numbers of ripe fruits appear and collecting becomes worthwhile. The gatherers avoid picking immature fruits (*caboasi*, "it is still green"). Poposáhuim ("between green and ripe") are collected and left to ripen in a bucket. Huásim (ripe fruits) are often eaten then and there.

In spite of the intense heat and humidity of late July and August, pitaya-gathering time is one of the happiest of the year in the Mayo region. The best collecting begins before sunup, before the birds, bees, and wasps plus a host of flies and gnats have managed to wreak havoc among the ripening fruits and before the heat and biting and buzzing insects become overwhelming.

Each collector, both men and women and occasionally young people, fashions a collecting spear called *jíabuia* in Mayo (*bacote* in Spanish). The jíabuia is often made from a quiote (flowering stalk) of a tall *cu'u* (*Agave angustifolia*) or, if that is not available, from the ribs of dead pitayas or etchos lashed together. For lower-growing fruits, the pitayero will cut a long limb of the leguminous *jócona* (*Havardia sonorae*), leaving a forked tip, which can be used to pry and wiggle off fruits and wedge them in the fork, thus preventing bruising by falling to the earth. (Bruised fruits spoil quickly.) For taller plants, a sharp point usually made from pisi (*R. thurberi*) is carefully lashed onto the end of the bacote. With the bacote resting on a shoulder, the gatherer, often accompanied by children, traipses off into the monte, looking alternately downward to check for thorns and rattlesnakes and upward to judge the merits of the pitayas. He or she evaluates the egg-sized fruits and carefully impales those considered to be ripe for picking, gently wriggles them from the cactus, and lowers them to the ground, where the fruits are delicately removed from the spear point.

Delicately, I say, because the spines can inflict pain, as I can attest.

On good collecting days the poposáhuim fruits are gathered into an *aca'ari* (gathering bucket) until it is full. These fruits are left till afternoon or even overnight, during which time the spines are said to soften, making peeling less hazardous to the fingers. Sometimes the spines simply fall off or are easily scraped away. At other times removing them requires more effort. For the uninitiated, scraping off the spines can be a messy, painful business. For Mayos, it is like drying dishes.

Older Mayos report that decades ago they would sling an aca'ari over their shoulders for collecting pitayas. This container is a cylinder open at the top, about 18 in. (45 cm) tall and 12 in. (30 cm) in diameter and built of pitaya ribs lashed together with a drumlike bottom of woven deer-hide strips. The top of the aca'ari is held rigid by a tightly lashed strip of *guásima* wood[81] steamed into a coil. The bucket is worn over the shoulder by a strap made of *ixtle* (fiber of *A. angustifolia*). Formerly, all Mayos would use aca'árim in harvest times, a large size for men, a smaller size for women. Now Mayos under forty years of age are unfamiliar with their use and their manufacture.*

On collecting forays, some pitayeros consume a large number of the fruits on the spot. Others save the best ones for home and exercise stern discipline by not selecting the most succulent ones for themselves. Other pitaye-

An *aca'ari*, a *pitaya*-gathering basket made by Serapio Gámez of San José de Masiaca, Sonora. (Drawing by Paul Mirocha)

ros hope to market the fruits, however, so they eat only damaged or unmarketable ones, and they save considerable time by simply plopping the fruits into the gathering bucket, not stopping to scrape off the spines.

Pitayeros, whether in the monte or at home, dexterously despine and peel the fruits without being pricked by the spines, which vary in the painfulness of their affliction from plant to plant. Around the villages the personalities of individual cacti are well known, and those with spines inflicting the most painful punctures are treated delicately. Novices must practice with many fruits before becoming proficient at peeling off the well-armed husks, avoiding both the long and short spines. Small children practice separating the fruits from the spines. By the time they have reached ten years of age, children are usually dexterous in harvesting and will eat the first few dozen fruits they collect. During pitaya season their hands, mouths, chins, and cheeks are usually stained pink from the fruit. So are mine, from fruits gathered by others, for I have never achieved proficiency at removing the spines.

The quality of the fruit varies from cactus to cactus, as does the color. Plants apparently bear the same color of fruits from year to year. The dominant color of the pulp is scarlet. Approximately 5 percent[82] of the plants of southern Sonora yield whitish pulp, called *zarca* (Spanish) or *tótosi* (Cáhita), which has a more delicate flavor. Occasionally (I have seen only three such plants) a pitaya yields fruits with orange husks and yellowish pulp. I tried one and found it to have a subtler flavor than the normal dark red variety. The best fruits are often said to be from those uncommon plants that produce fruits of guinda, a bright purple pulp. I know of but one such plant, which is oddly shaped (branches growing every

---

* Because they are constructed from organ pipe parts, it is illegal under the Convention on the Importation of Threatened and Endangered Species to import *aca'árim* or any wild cactus or cactus part into the United States.

which way), though Mayos have assured me that they are to be found here and there. The fruits are somewhat larger and sweeter than average.

The number and size of fruits borne on the cacti varies considerably from year to year. In 2004 (an extraordinarily dry year) at Organ Pipe Cactus National Monument, the fruit crop was only 10 percent of normal.[83] Mayos say that drought years result in fewer and smaller fruits, and I was able to verify this in my field studies (1995–2001). In summer 2001, following a nearly rainless spring and a dry previous summer, large portions of the pitaya forests bore few, if any, fruits. In one village, community development workers lamented to me that due to lack of fruit they were forced to cancel a workshop on producing pitaya preserves. Other villages also had below-normal harvests. The lack of income from sale of the fruits made for considerable hardship among the poorer Mayos of El Pitayal that year. Most of them live in adobe or mud-and-daub houses with earthen floors and no running water. The few dollars earned each day from selling pitayas make a major contribution to their economic well-being during the late summer. Droughts are especially painful to those nearest the earth.

Most years, natives of the region and throughout Sonora gather the fruits and sell them in local markets. Yaquis regularly congregate near a checkpoint along the International Highway, where vehicles must stop for inspection. There they offer freshly gathered and despined fruits. I have seen them become quite creative in marketing: some would hold a rope across the highway and urge the motorists that dutifully stopped to purchase pitayas and make a donation to the Yaquis. (They were quite adept at dropping the rope at the last possible second when motorists refused to halt.) The rope trick didn't last long, but the pitaya sellers remained and are there every July and August offering the delectable fruits.

Street vendors often hawk the fruits at traffic stoplights or at other tollbooths and checkpoints along the highway. In summer 2004 despined pitayas sold for three pesos (30 cents) each. In central Sonora, gatherers carry their harvest up to 60 mi. (100 km) to the state capital of Hermosillo. In each Mayo village several people are busy during the harvest season gathering the fruits, at times selling them to a local buyer, who, in turn, markets them in the cities. For several hundred individuals in Sonora, collecting and selling pitayas is a vital source of income. Once the spines have been removed, however, the fruits ripen rapidly and usually last no more than twenty-four hours before rotting. The husks soften and putrefying liquid runs out. Commercial producers in southern Mexico ship pitayas with the spines intact, which, they say, retards ripening. The short shelf life of pitayas is a serious blockage to commercial production in Sonora, where harvest-season temperatures are considerably higher than those of southern Mexico.

The rinds (or husks) of pitayas are edible, unlike those of most other columnar cacti.[84] Mayos do not eat them, however, and I have not tried. Where villagers harvest the fruits, they save the husks and feed them to pigs and goats, an important source of fodder for animals belonging to these impoverished rural folk. I have watched livestock eating the husks and am amazed that they seem to be unfazed by the spines, for even the best pitayero usually leaves a few small hard spines that stubbornly adhere to the rind along the point of attachment to the branch.

It is not only livestock that benefit from the harvest. In Sirebampo one family of pitayeros maintains a large pile of heavy scrap metal near their house. Several years ago a clan of large spiny-tailed iguanas (Ctenosaura hemilopha) took up residence in the pile. These fierce lizards, which can inflict nasty bites, grow to more than 18 in. (45 cm) in length. They spend much of their days basking in the sunlight. In summer, family members and guests toss pitaya husks toward the metal pile, and the lizards lumber out to feast on tiny morsels of fruit left on the husks, then go to work on the husks.

In addition to producing fruits, organ pipes are an important source of lumber. The lower wood of the trunk and arms of the pitaya cactus is surprisingly tough and sturdy. Saddle-makers use it to form the wooden base for saddles. Many years ago Mayos and Yaquis discovered how to use the wood in many phases of

Fence and home built of *pitaya* ribs, Huebampo, Sonora. The roof is made of compacted dirt with
a row of adobe bricks as protection against strong winds.

house building, including crossbeams that bear heavy weights. Traditional houses in the Mayo lowlands usually have roofs of stripped pitaya branches over which slats of split branches are laid perpendicularly. On top the builders usually place a layer of grass or dense herbage that is then covered with adobe. Often these mud roofs support growth of grasses and weeds that dissipate the energy of pounding rain and prolong the life of the roof. These roofs are far more efficient insulators than the concrete roofs more popular among non-Mayos and non-Yaquis. The thick layer of dirt keeps the house cool in summer and warm in winter. However, such a roof is usually associated with poverty or rural life, and thus considered a mark of low social status. Along the coastal plain from Huatabampo south into Sinaloa, the walls of many homes are made of interwoven pitaya arms, often harvested green and woven while still pliable.

In most rural Mayo communities, pitaya branches are the preferred material for fences (chinámim), walls, ceilings, and even some furniture. For fencing, the flesh is chopped away with a machete. When the woody remnants have dried for a few days, they are split and then woven in and out among a couple of strands of plain wire. Thus worked, the branches produce dense fencing that is attractive and effective, affording privacy as well as protection. Such fences are livestock-proof, an important consideration in a region where livestock roam freely and can destroy a garden and landscape plants in only a few minutes. Most Mayo kitchens are also out of doors and marauding burros and goats can

A *chinami*, a fence of split *pitaya* branches, Jambiolobampo, Sonora.

handily upset a table, smash and break utensils, and finish off home-cooked food, while a cow can trample any number of important items and household and garden plants. (Pigs uprooted and savaged a garden belonging to some friends, who had invested nearly a month's work in it.) Mayos also prefer to live apart from other families, and the chinami, in addition to affording protection, expresses well their love of privacy, shielding them from potentially prying eyes.

No plant functions better for constructing living fences. Prior to the mid-1950s, when barbed wire became available and affordable in rural Sonora, large numbers of organ pipe cuttings were planted in rows, often mixed with cuttings of etchos, to produce living fences. As the fences matured they became useful as barriers but also as sources of pitaya fruits. A few of these producing groves still grow along back roads near villages in the Mayo region. A fence that doubles as an orchard is a double asset.* Older observers warn that for cuttings to take root, they should be cut in late winter in the cool weather and allowed to sit for a week or two. These observations appear to be true, for in an experiment in a Mayo village, workers and I discovered to our dismay that cuttings planted in May and June mostly failed to take root or were dormant for over a year before sprouting. More than half of them died.

The dried wood is used in great quantities as fuel for ovens, for baking bread, and in kilns for firing burnt adobes. Andrés Pérez de Ribas, writing in the mid-

---

* Columnar cacti, including several species of *Stenocereus*, are popular for fencing throughout Mexico. Most commonly used is the straight-growing Mexican fence cactus (also called *malinche*), *Pachycereus marginatus*, widely planted in the states of Guerrero, Hidalgo, Mexico, Oaxaca, Puebla, and Querétaro. In these areas stacks of cuttings for fence building are a common sight.

Ceiling of *pitaya* branches, Loma de Angeles, Masiaca, Sonora.

seventeenth century, observed that on chilly winter nights, natives of the region would gather ribs for heating:

> On some of the bitter nights of the two coldest months of the year (. . . December and January), they use firebrands, which they light and place in the cold sand next to them. They use this means of warmth when they travel through uninhabited regions, placing the firebrands in a row, each a short distance from the next (wood is never lacking because of the many *montes* in this province). They lie down to sleep between the firebrands and take care to extinguish them when they awake. Lastly, if one of these scantily dressed Indians wants to travel four or six leagues at night in spite of the intense cold, he takes a burning firebrand in his hands and places it near his stomach for warmth, leaving the rest of the body exposed to the wind.[85]

Many tons of dead branches are still gathered throughout the region to fuel burnt adobe manufacture. Large portions of El Pitayal have become devoid of dead plants—and the myriad creatures that inhabit the senescent and dead plants. Recently, live plants have been felled and left to dry as a future source of fuel.

The organ pipe has medical uses as well. The fleshy, moist stem is singed to remove the spines and then applied directly to the flesh for snake and insect bites, a remedy that I tested with positive results when an assassin bug bit my colleague, ecologist Tom Van Devender. Many Mayos recommend placing a chunk of flesh on the bites of *jovari*, the common and irritable black harvester ants.[86] Other Mayos reported that the scorched peel of the fruit is applied directly to the anus for hemorrhoids, rightly cautioning that it must first be scorched enough to burn off the spines. In one village, dried peels (*aaqui begua*) are boiled

Home completely surrounded by a *chinami*, Jambiolobampo, Sonora.

into a tea that is taken for bad stomach and to stop hemorrhaging in women.

An odd use of the cactus came to me through a Mayo friend in southern Sonora. He noted that the smoke from burning pitaya branches would neutralize the musk sprayed from a skunk. His procedure for cleansing a sprayed dog was to close the wretched creature in a room and build a small fire of the pitaya ribs inside the room, then let it smolder. He swore that the smoke, if it reached all the affected areas of the animal, would eliminate the powerful stench of skunk musk. I have never had an opportunity to test his claim and would worry about the potential asphyxiation of the poor brute.

A crested form of the organ pipe cactus, a curiosity called *aaqui nábera*, appears sporadically throughout the region. Crests, also called fasciations, appear in numerous species of cacti and in other plants as well. What causes these oddly appealing malformations is not known. An aaqui nábera often yields no fruit. When it does, traditional Mayos warn that the fruits should not be eaten. The malformed plant is bad, they say, and the fruit is thus contaminated. Some

more intrepid folk disregard such warnings and eat the fruits anyway.

Scattered throughout the indigenous Mayo Comunidad de Masiaca in southern Sonora is found an apparent hybrid cactus, perhaps a cross between the organ pipe and the *sina* (*S. alamosensis*).[87] It is a columnar cactus up to 17 ft. (5 m) tall, with curling branches, but with reddish pink tubular flowers instead of the whitish symmetrical blooms of pitayas. The fruits are sweet and juicy, though small, similar to those of the sina. The dried branches are hollow, and the wood is hard and durable. The Mayos refer to the plant by the hybrid name *sinaaqui*. The plants produce far fewer fruits than the pitaya, and natives do not view them as important fruit producers.

For the Seris, until recently a nomadic people who now inhabit an arid section of Sonora's northern coastline, the organ pipe (*ool*, the *l* pronounced like the Nahuatl *tl*) was nearly as important as for the Mayos. Seris formerly ranged far inland, but from the beginning of the twentieth century were largely confined to the coast and a few miles inland and to islands in the Gulf of California,

Vicente Tajia next to a crested *pitaya*, Coteco, Sonora.
Some Mayos warn against eating any fruits from such plants.

primarily Tiburón and San Esteban Islands. Perhaps 700 Seris live in two permanent villages on the Sea of Cortés in some of the world's finest cactus habitat.

When I first came to know the Seris in the late 1960s, pitaya fruits were one of their favorite foods. Small groups would routinely march into the desert to eat their fill and bring back buckets of the red fruits. Gathering and consumption of the pitaya dulce has decreased dramatically in the last two decades, however. In 1999 I drove several traditional Seris into the monte near El Desemboque, the more northern of their two villages, and was saddened to learn that they had not harvested

cactus fruits for nearly two years. They reported that, with their increased cash income, it was easier to purchase processed food in the village stores or in Kino Bay, and no one wanted to drive them on harvesting trips any more. The fruits (*ool imam*), so enthusiastically and extensively gathered when I first knew the Seris, are now only infrequently and, I fear, casually harvested.

The Seris would also dry the fruits but never on a large scale, probably because even with an annual rainfall of fewer than 5 in. (12.5 cm) annually, the humidity along the coast during the harvest season was often oppressively high. They were rather more successful than Mayos

Vicente Tajia stands behind a *sinaaqui*, an apparent hybrid, possibly between *Stenocereus alamosensis* and *S. martinezii*, Masiaca Indigenous Community, Sonora.

at this, however. In the south the humidity is always stifling in the pitaya fruiting season.

Seris had numerous additional uses for pitaya dulce. Dead plants were subjected to a labor-intensive process that produced caulking compound, especially useful for their boats.[88] One specific cultural exploitation I ran upon quite by chance in 1980 was the use of the cactus during a puberty festival. The entire village participated in the two-day ceremony honoring a young woman who had come of age. A *pascola* (ceremonial dancer) tapped out a complex rhythm with his heels on a small dance platform, while a singer shook a rattle and accompanied the dancer with a seemingly unending string of songs. The men gathered in one spot and gambled. The women,

completely apart, played a game in which perhaps fifteen of them sat on the ground in a wide circle and passed around several narrow cross sections of pitaya dulce branches, which acted as pieces in a game with complicated rules. The game lasted for many hours.[89]

The pitaya dulce was also a prominent plant in Baja California cultures, as well as to the Hia Ced O'odham (Sand Papago) of southwestern Arizona and northwestern Sonora.[90] The Hia Ced O'odham live in the driest and hottest region of North America, including the Pinacate Volcanic region, and they developed techniques for drying and storing pitaya dulce fruits, establishing caches and relying on them for emergencies or when traveling across broad stretches of barren terrain.

Organ Pipe Fruits as a Commercial Crop

In pockets of northern Sonora, exploitation of pitayas has replaced grazing of livestock as a source of income. The railroad town of Carbó, some 40 mi. (65 km) north of the state capital of Hermosillo, is home to fine stands of organ pipes whose fruits ripen from late June through mid-August. For unknown reasons, Carbó pitayas are larger and generally sweeter than those of any other region. Pitayeros market them in the crowded streets of Hermosillo. Residents produce preserves and dried pitaya fruits and eat the fresh fruits as well.

Pitayeros from Carbó usually make their way to the International Highway at El Oasis, where they hitch rides or flag down local buses to Hermosillo and its large market. I gave one such pitayero a ride along with his five-gallon bucketful of delectable fruit. He reported that eighty Carbó residents pick pitayas for the market for between two and three months each year. On good days they can earn in excess of $100 from sales in Hermosillo. Out of curiosity, I accompanied the fellow when he disembarked in Hermosillo, and his pitayas immediately attracted public interest. I understood why when I purchased a few from him and consider the fruits so valuable that they refrain from eating them. Such self-restraint is admirable but lamentable, for the fruits are surely far more nutritious than soda pop or other sugary beverages that are both heavily consumed and expensive.

On June 30 and July 1 Carbó celebrates its annual Pitaya Festival. During the festivities residents elect a queen and sponsor a parade. Awards are given for a delightful variety of categories: largest pitaya, prettiest pitaya, best-flavored pitaya popsicle, most attractive color, sweetest, oddest shape, and so on. In 2004 the largest weighed in at 400 g, nearly a pound.

In the cities of Hermosillo, Ciudad Obregón, and Navojoa pitaya harvesters sell the fruits in markets, at traffic lights, and door to door. Mayos from Sirebampo rise before daybreak during the fruiting season and harvest plastic bucketsful of pitayas. They lug the laden buckets to the bus stop, 2 km away, and ride the bus to Navojoa, 45 km to the northwest. They sell all the fruits, about 100 to a bucketful, and return with groceries and clothing they purchase with the receipts.

Some families in Sirebampo now produce *mermelada de pitaya* (pitaya jam). Entire families join in the process, which involves boiling many bucketsful of pitayas on outdoor stoves (most cooking in Mayo villages is done out of doors on wood fires), adding a thickener like pectin, skimming off the froth, and pouring the resul-

Pitayas from Carbó, in central Sonora. These large fruits are in great demand in markets in the Sonoran capital of Hermosillo.

tant liquid into jars fitted with appropriate seals. Quality control is critical for this venture, since the water content of the fruits varies. If the cooks boil the fruits too long, they are cooking away their profits; if not long enough, the product will be more like syrup. Some cooks have found that adding sugar makes the syrup more workable, acts as a preservative, and makes the mixture a little less slimy (cactus fruits have considerable mucilage content).

Mayos have no difficulty selling the jam locally, but the high cost of canning jars and the difficulty of controlling the moisture content have proved to be problems. One batch was pretty well ruined when it was prepared on a day with shifting winds that blew smoke in and out of the kettle, producing a strange smoky flavor. Still, the jam has a delicious taste. In the summer La Michoacana, a national Mexican chain that sells ice cream and fruit bars called *paletas*, offers one of pitaya flavor.

Although cultivation of the pitaya for commercial orchards is an important industry in southern Mexico, it is in its infancy in Sonora. No one has undertaken such commercialization at Carbó. The orchards recently planted in El Pitayal are too young to bear fruits. They are growing rapidly, however, and by the year 2010 the organ pipes should be producing. While it is a promising industry, the years required for maturity of the plants are a long time for people who live in poverty.

Seven

The Future of Organ Pipes

ORGAN PIPES FORTUNATE enough to live and grow in the United States seem relatively safe for the moment. Most of them lie within Organ Pipe Cactus National Monument and Cabeza Prieta National Wildlife Refuge. The rest grow primarily on tribal lands (Tohono O'odham) and on lands administered by federal and state governments where, in theory, they are afforded statutory protection. Only a few are found on private lands subject to development, and those few are a recognized asset whose owners are usually inclined to protect them.

In Mexico, however, the organ pipe is far more vulnerable. In the north, countless thousands have fallen as ranchers have bulldozed desert vegetation—more than 2 million acres (800,000 ha) of it—to make way for the planting of savannah-like grasses, primarily buffelgrass (*Pennisetum ciliare*), an introduced African grass that increases beef production. An even larger portion of Sonora has been semicleared and seeded with the grass. Buffelgrass craves fire, sprouting immediately afterward and growing quickly, whereas fire kills Sonoran Desert vegetation, including vast numbers of pitayas. A Sonoran rancher recently reported to me that some cattle ranchers have abandoned buffelgrass planting and are protecting and cultivating pitayas as a potentially greater source of income than beef. This is a hopeful report indeed, but now that buffelgrass has been established, it is here to stay. We can no more eliminate it than we can starlings or crabgrass. It continues to expand its range and remains a threat to native vegetation due to its aggressive growth and its fondness for the fire that is lethal to other plants.

An even greater threat faces El Pitayal. In spite of the beauty and the demonstrated economic value of this forest, Mexican government officials have long urged the Mayos, on whose ancestral lands much of El Pitayal lies, to lease the lands to agribusinesses. When that happens, of course, clearing away the pitayas and leveling the land is never far behind. Even small clearings may sound the death knell to pitayas. In August 1999 a group of comuneros of Masiaca cleared a 100-acre (40-ha) parcel of dense pitaya forest for pasture. They left behind a few solitary cacti. Fires set to burn the slash lethally scorched most of these. By the following fall the remainder had perished due to full exposure to sunlight. I estimate that more than 2000 mature pitayas were destroyed in the operation.

That operation was a tiny one. In December 1999 nearly all the land of the mestizo-owned Ejido Melchor Ocampo to the south—more than 3750 acres (1500 ha) of El Pitayal—was bulldozed and leveled in the hope that water for irrigation would arrive. Based on average densities in the region, the operation likely killed more than 200,000 mature pitayas.

In 2000 bulldozers cleared 1250 acres (500 ha) of prime pitaya habitat on Sonora's southern coast designated for shrimp farming by a surveying mistake. Today those lands lie empty, with only low-lying, shrubby plants growing where the organ pipe forest had been. In 2001 private investors announced plans to bulldoze an additional 12,500 acres (5000 ha) of pitaya forest to make way for shrimp farms along the same coast. Each of these installations requires about 1200 acres (480 ha), and standard installation procedures require that the land be leveled and stripped of all plants. When the economic life of the shrimping operation ends (usually

after about five years) the wasteland left behind is a source of blowing dirt, sand, and little else. These plans were still pending in 2004, and the Sonoran and Mexican governments continue to promote shrimp farming as a source of economic development.

To what extent the destruction of so many organ pipes will harm our small U.S. population cannot yet be determined. However, the Sonoran pitayas are clearly a vast food reservoir for migrating pollinators, including hummingbirds and several species of bats, but above all for the nectar-feeding lesser long-nosed bat (*Leptonycteris curasoae*). This remarkable bat is the primary pollinator of Sonoran columnar cacti. It relies on the nectar of flowers offered by the huge populations of Sonoran columnar cacti for its food source during its migrations up the coast of Mexico to maternity wards in southern Arizona and environs.[91] As the bats rely on the cactus nectar for energy and food, so the cacti rely to a great extent on the bats for pollination. The loss of substantial numbers of either party—pollinator or nectar producer—would necessarily affect the other partner in the symbiotic relationship. The disappearance of huge numbers of pitayas will inevitably impinge on pollinator populations and their ability to continue their migratory patterns. Just as the lack of pitaya fruits hindered the migration of Baja Californians, the lack of nectar may hinder the migrations of lesser long-nosed bats. In the absence of migratory pollinators, the ability of organ pipes in the United States to reproduce successfully will likely be compromised and future populations jeopardized. The health of organ pipes in Organ Pipe National Monument is surely linked to the health of migratory bats in Mexico.

There are enormous numbers of pitayas in Sonora, and they seem to endure rather well the onslaught of increased human population. However, such range "improvement" projects and clearings for irrigated agriculture and shrimp farms continue to decimate the most important populations. Already nearly half of the densest part of El Pitayal has been cleared, most of it since the mid-1980s. By any measure of biological and aesthetic uniqueness, the El Pitayal is worthy of

The Zacate Blanco Pitaya Reserve, Coteco, Sonora.

becoming a national park. Unfortunately for the pitayas and the native peoples who use them, the agricultural and aquacultural schemes proposed in the region place little value on the pitayas and their habitat. Only when Mexicans can demonstrate the pitayas' true worth in pesos and the small-time users who know their value achieve political power will the plants be safe.

These are examples of problems faced by those who wish to preserve the organ pipe forests, including many Mayos. In 2000 and 2001 my associates and I worked with groups within the Masiaca Comunidad (where the densest remaining forests are found) and nongovernmental organizations from the United States to establish two small reserves of 63 acres (25 ha) and 500 acres (200 ha). We provided money for fencing, and men from

cooperatives that own the land built the fences. Realizing that excluding cattle and goats from the reserves would mean a loss of income for the pastoralists, we have also regularly reimbursed the cooperatives for revenues they have lost.

Setting up the reserves was not as smooth a process as I had hoped. Work was held up briefly when a tiny group of comuneros, including the commissioner of the community, opposed the project, primarily because we refused to pay them a bribe. The commissioner presented a written complaint to the national Department of Agrarian Reform, accusing me of stealing cacti from El Pitayal and taking them to the United States. I confessed to the investigating authority that over a period of months I had indeed eaten hundreds of fruits in El

Pitayal, but the amount I carried out in my digestive tract was the extent of my export activities. Given the strict enforcement of laws against the export of cacti and cactus parts from Mexico, I was hardly likely to be smuggling such plants into the United States, especially when plants raised from seeds are readily available and inexpensive at cactus nurseries in Arizona. The investigator gave a wry smile and took notes. The comuneros in favor of the project soon overwhelmed the few objectors, however, and the work on the fences continued. Meanwhile, we recruited local people to protect and monitor the reserves. Since that time I have received numerous requests from other comuneros to create more reserves, but funding has not been available.

While establishing the protected areas, we worked with adjacent Mayo villages to organize the commercial marketing of pitaya fruits and fruit products as a way of generating local income. We presented programs in local schools, encouraging older Mayos to underscore the importance of El Pitayal to children, educating them the same way they educated us outsiders. Finally, we contacted local ecotourism companies and urged them to include the reserves on their list of places to visit, hoping that increased visitation and income would provide additional incentives for impoverished local residents to maintain the integrity of El Pitayal. Some of these efforts have worked and some have not. After four years of workshops, however, several families were busy during the pitaya harvest season churning out pitaya jam and pitaya seca. It is my hope that others will see the opportunities and join us in sharing with the world the pleasure of organ pipe cactus fruits and participate in the effort to preserve this remarkable habitat and the forest of organ pipes it perpetuates.

Notes

1. I rely on Pennington (1980) for this name. Although I have inquired about other terms in several former Nébome towns, I have been informed universally that the only name for the plant and fruit is *pitaya*. Pitayas are abundant in the upper reaches of the Sahuaripa Valley, which includes the Mountain Pima towns of Onapa and Guisamopa. Reina Guerrero (1993) did not mention a common name for *Stenocereus thurberi* in her ethnobotanical study among the Pimas of the municipality of Yécora, whose boundaries do not include the abovementioned towns (they are included in the municipality of Sahuaripa).

2. Castetter and Underhill (1935, 37).

3. Rea (1997, 282).

4. Whoever applied the name *organ pipe*, however, had not seen the *sahuira* of mountainous southeastern Sonora or the *chico* (*Pachycereus weberi*) of southern Mexico, both of which more closely resemble organ pipes. Branches of organ pipe plants in southern Sonora often run every which way.

5. Susan Rutman of Organ Pipe Cactus National Monument brought this point to my attention.

6. The other two are the saguaro in Saguaro National Park in Arizona and the *cardón pasacana* (*Trichocereus atacamensis*) in Los Cardones National Park in the province of Salta, Argentina.

7. López Pérez (1999, 127).

8. Turner et al. (1995) reported sporadic individual plants as far south as Guasave, Sinaloa. In 2003 I found organ pipes growing in healthy numbers even farther south, on hillsides roughly 25 mi. (40 km) northwest of Culiacán. Other researchers report robust populations near Cosalá.

9. I follow here the vegetation classification used in Martin et al. (1998).

10. Axelrod (1979); Van Devender (2002).

11. Van Devender (2002, 15).

12. Van Devender (1987).

13. *Etcho* is the Cáhita (Mayo and Yaqui) name for the cactus. Elsewhere it is usually called *cardón*. The name cardón (meaning "big thistle") is commonly used to denote several columnar cacti species. It is the name originally given by Spaniards to many columnars in North and South America.

14. In the Plains of Sonora subdivision of the Sonoran Desert, as classified by Shreve (Shreve and Wiggins 1964), organ pipes are extremely common and saguaros limited in numbers. Saguaros may find it difficult to obtain adequate light within the often dense growth of ironwood and other trees.

15. This is the boundary offered by Forrest Shreve as the result of his intense scrutiny of climate and vegetation of the region. This limit is now rather useless, because nearly all the adjacent vegetation has been cleared for irrigated farming. Where the native vegetation resumes, however, now some distance to the southeast, the change is dramatic and warrants exclusion from the Sonoran Desert. See Shreve and Wiggins (1964).

16. Hastings and Turner (1965, 17a).

17. Broyles (1996).

18. The genera *Pereskia* and *Pereskiopsis* both have fully developed leaves and are considered ancestral to nearly all other cacti, which number roughly 1800 species.

19. Felger (2000, 226).

20. Gibson and Nobel (1986, 9).

21. For a discussion of CAM metabolism, see Gibson and Nobel (1986, 9).

22. Bowen (2000, 469).

23. S. Rutman, personal communication, 2005.

24. The relevant vegetation types of southern Sonora and northern Sinaloa along a coast-to-mountain gradient are coastal thornscrub, foothills thornscrub, and tropical deciduous forest.

25. Data are from Bustamante (2003).

26. Terms are from Gibson (1990).

27. Ongoing studies of growth rates, flowering and fruiting sequences, and plant productivity are being conducted in El Pitayal by Alberto Búrquez and Enriquena Bustamante of the Centro de Ecología, Universidad Nacional Autónoma de México, Hermosillo.

28. Several Mayo consultants have known individual plants for decades and are thus in a position to estimate their age.

29. Enriquena Bustamante, personal communication, 2005. She measured 185 individual plants near Sonoita, Sonora, across the border from Organ Pipe Cactus National Monument, and 93 plants within El Pitayal.

30. Parker (1988, 343).

31. In 2004 one of the cuttings flowered and developed a fruit, which failed to mature. My interpretation of the flowering is that the plant has the genetic age sufficient for flowering and acts according to that age, not according to the time in the ground.

32. Parker (1987, 295).

33. Bustamante (2003).

34. Parker (1988, 341); more specifically, mean stem growth increased as winter precipitation increased and freeze frequency decreased. Also, S. Rutman, personal communication, 2005.

35. Hastings and Turner (1965, 14).

36. Bustamante (2003) suggested that the nearly complete absence of juveniles in her study sites probably indicates episodic germination, that is, germination occurs only when a series of climate variables occurs in the appropriate sequence. While I suspect that she is correct, the hypothesis is complicated by many young plants growing on a gentle ridge of apparently sandy soil several miles long. Juveniles of varied ages grow there. Neither of us has an explanation for this phenomenon.

37. Fleming (2002, 208).

38. Bustamante (2003).

39. Bustamante (2003, 70). Counting the tiny seeds from many fruits requires true scientific dedication.

40. Fleming (2002, 208).

41. Felger and Moser (1985, 258).

42. Sahley (2001).

43. Fleming (2002, 208).

44. W. Peachey, personal communication, 2000.

45. In *Stenocereus griseus* of Venezuela, ingestion by bats or birds increases the probability of germination from 75 to 86 percent and decreases germination time from 28 to 15 days (Naranjo et al. 2003).

46. Yar Petryszyn, personal communication, 2005.

47. I have noted numerous individuals of an apparently undescribed species of *Stenocereus* along the Pacific Coast of Guerrero and Oaxaca. A second apparently undescribed species appears in portions of the southern valleys of Oaxaca. Both species become enormous, reaching more than 40 ft. (12 m) in height.

48. *Stenocereus stellatus* is widely called *xoconochtli*, *S. treleasei* is *tunillo*, *S. alamosensis* is *sina*, and *S. chrysocarpus* is *pachón*.

49. See Cornejo (1994) for a discussion of this phenomenon.

50. Gibson (1990).

51. This phenomenon in organ pipes was first brought to my attention by Richard Felger, personal communication, ca. 1998.

52. Gibson and Norak (1978, 1037).

53. In 2002 I photographed a *Stenocereus* in Zopilote Canyon in the state of Guerrero. I found the plant puzzling, because it was different from any other *Stenocereus*, yet similar enough that I took it to be a variant of *S. stellatus*. I learned to my delight that in 2004 Mexican researchers described it as *S. zopilotensis*, a new species (Arreola-Nava and Terrazas 2004).

54. *Stenocereus alamosensis* (*sina*), *S. gummosus* (*pitaya agria*), *S. thurberi* (*pitaya*), and *S. montanus* (*sahuira*).

55. Felger et al. (1992).

56. Rea (1997, 282).

57. See, for example, Yetman and Van Devender (2002).

58. All are members of Fabaceae, the bean family: *mezquite*, primarily *Prosopis glandulosa*; ironwood, *Olneya tesota*; *jócona*, *Havardia sonorae*; *mimosa*, primarily *Mimosa distachya*.

59. Obregón (1584 [1997], 153).

60. Pfefferkorn (1989, 75–76).

61. Hodgson (2001, 142).

62. Hodgson (2001, 142).

63. del Barco (1980, 149).

64. Crosby (1994, 213).

65. Alanís (1998, 5); translation mine.

66. Hodgson (2001, 143).

67. Och (1965, 155).

68. Cited from Fontana (1980, 66).

69. Arbelaez (1991).

70. Castetter and Underhill (1935, 22).

71. Underhill (1946, 154).

72. Rea (1997, 283).

73. Aschmann (1952).

74. Aschmann (1952, 77); Alanís (1998).

75. Felger and Moser (1985, 253).

76. del Barco (1981, 75).

77. See also Yetman and Van Devender (2001).

78. The term is derogatory, even when used by indigenous people, who at times refer to very poor or frequently drunk individuals as *indios*.

79. Fruits of the *tetecho* (*Neobuxbaumia tetetzo*), a close cousin of the saguaro found in the Valle de Techuacán in the Mexican state of Pueblo, also split open and dry while still attached to the plant, whereas pitayas do not.

80. Ópatas, a name given by Spaniards to several groups including Tegüimas and Eudeves, were the principal indigenous group of northeastern Sonora at the time of the Conquest. By the early twentieth century, they were extinct as a people.

81. *Guásima* (*Guazuma ulmifolia* Sterculiaceae; *ágiya* in Cáhita) is an important tree of dry tropical forests and is common in the tropical deciduous forest and thornscrub of northwestern Mexico.

82. This figure is based on a count I made of hundreds of pitayas gathered for processing into preserves at the Mayo village of Sirebampo, Sonora.

83. S. Rutman, personal communication, 2005.

84. Felger and Moser (1985, 258).

85. Pérez de Ribas (1999, 89). He may have been referring to the ribs of *Stenocereus montanus*, which is more common in the Río Fuerte uplands than is *S. thurberi*.

86. Cozárit M. (1985).

87. Ecologist Alberto Búrquez (personal communication, 2003) believes the plant is a hybrid cross between *Stenocereus alamosensis* and *S. martinezii*, which is found in central Sinaloa south into Colima.

88. Felger and Moser (1985, 258).

89. Additional uses of *ool* were enumerated comprehensively by Felger and Moser (1985).

90. Hodgson (2001).

91. Fleming (2002).

Glossary

aguas, las. Sonoran term for summer rains.

areolar (glandular) **trichomes.** Areoles that are gummy or resinous.

areoles. Wartlike growths on the ribs of branches of columnar cacti from which spines emerge.

caboasi. Mayo term for immature pitaya fruits.

Cáhita. The language of Mayos and Yaquis; it means "there is nothing."

chinami, chinámim. Mayo term for fence(s) constructed of dried and split organ pipe branches.

coastal thornscrub. Plant community along the southern coast of Sonora characterized by many species of cacti and a thick growth of drought-tolerant short trees and bushes.

comuneros. Members of Mexican indigenous communities.

El Pitayal. Local name for the dense organ pipe forest of southern Sonora.

equipatas. Sonoran term for winter rains.

etcho. Columnar cactus, *Pachycereus pecten-aboriginum*; also called *cardón.*

foothills thornscrub. Plant community of central to southern Sonora characterized by numerous short trees and large shrubs, many with thorns.

huásim. Mayo term for ripe pitaya fruits.

monte. The bush, natural vegetation.

paposáhuim. Mayo term for pitaya fruits that are between green and ripe.

pitaya. Organ pipe fruit; in Sonora, also the plant.

pitaya dulce. Common name in northern Sonora for the organ pipe.

pitaya seca. Dried organ pipe fruit.

pitayal. Any area of unusual concentration of organ pipe cacti.

pitayero (a). Organ pipe fruit picker.

pitayo. Name widely given to the organ pipe and its relatives.

pitire. Columnar cactus of Michoacán, *Stenocereus quevedonis*.

saguaro. Columnar cactus of the Sonoran Desert, *Carnegiea gigantea*.

sahueso. Columnar cactus of the Sonoran Gulf Coast and Baja California, *Pachycereus pringlei*; also called *cardón*.

sahuira. Large columnar cactus of southeastern Sonora, *Stenocereus montanus*.

sinita, senita. Columnar cactus of the greater Sonoran Desert, *Lophocereus schottii*.

thornscrub. Plant community of densely placed, low-lying trees and tall shrubs, many of which bear thorns.

tropical deciduous forest. Plant community of Mexico's West Coast extending well into Sonora, characterized by short trees that drop their leaves in response to the winter-spring drought and in which the tops of the tallest trees exceed the tops of the tallest columnar cacti.

yato. Common name in the Caribbean for *Stenocereus griseus*.

References

Alanís, G. L. 1998. *La pitahaya en la cultura del Noroeste*. Provincias Internas, Revista del Programa de Historia y Cultura Regional del Instituto de Investigaciones Económicas y Sociales de la Universidad Autónoma de Sinaloa. Vol. 1, no. 1, Winter 1998.

Arbelaez, María Soledad. 1991. The Sonoran missions and Indian raids of the eighteenth century. *Journal of the Southwest* 33:366–77.

Arreola-Nava, H., and T. Terrazas. 2004. A new species from Mexico. *Brittonia* 56:96–100.

Aschmann, H. 1952. A primitive food preparation technique in Baja California. *Southwestern Journal of Anthropology* 8:36–69.

Axelrod, D. 1979. Age and origin of the Sonoran Desert. *California Academy of Sciences Occasional Paper* 132, 1–74.

Bowen, T. 2000. *Unknown Island: Seri Indians, Europeans, and San Esteban Island in the Gulf of California*. Albuquerque: University of New Mexico Press.

Broyles, W. 1996. *Organ Pipe Cactus National Monument: Where Edges Meet*. Tucson: Southwest Parks and Monuments Association.

Bustamante, E. 2003. Variación espacial y temporal en la reproducción y estructura poblacional de *Stenocereus thurberi*: Una cactácea columnar del matorral costero del sur de Sonora, México. Unpublished M.A. thesis, Universidad Nacional Autónoma de México.

Castetter, Edward, and Ruth Underhill. 1935. *Ethnobotany of the Papago Indians*. University of New Mexico Bulletin 275, Biological Series, vol. 4, no. 3.

Cornejo, Dennis O. 1994. Morphological evolution and biogeography of Mexican columnar cacti, tribe Pachycereeae, Cactaceae. Unpublished Ph.D. dissertation, University of Texas, Austin.

Cozárit M., Ismael. 1985. *Medicina tradicional Mayo*. Hermosillo, Sonora: Dirección General de Culturas Populares.

Crosby, H. 1994. *Antigua California: Mission and Colony on the Peninsular Frontier, 1697–1768*. Albuquerque: University of New Mexico Press.

del Barco, M. 1980. *Natural History of Baja California (Historia natural y crónica de la Antigua California)*. Part 1. Translated by F. Tiscareno. Los Angeles: Dawson's Book Shop.

———. 1981. *Ethnology and Linguistics of Baja California (Historia natural y crónica de la Antigua California)*. Part 2. Translated by F. Tiscareno. Los Angeles: Dawson's Book Shop.

Felger, Richard. 2000. *Flora of the Gran Desierto and Río Colorado of Northwestern Mexico*. Tucson: University of Arizona Press.

Felger, Richard, and Mary Beck Moser. 1985. *People of the Desert and Sea: Ethnobotany of the Seri Indians*. Tucson: University of Arizona Press.

Felger, Richard, Peter Warren, Susan Anderson, and Gary Nabhan. 1992. Vascular plants of a desert oasis: Flora and ethnobotany of Quitobaquito, Organ Pipe Cactus National Monument, Arizona. *Proceedings of the San Diego Society of Natural History* 8:1–39.

Fleming, T. 2002. Pollination biology of four columnar cacti of the Sonoran Desert. In T. Fleming and A. Valiente-Banuet, editors, *Columnar Cacti and Their Mutualists*, 207–24. Tucson: University of Arizona Press.

Fontana, Bernard. 1980. Ethnobotany of the saguaro: An annotated bibliography. *Desert Plants* 2:61–78.

Gibson, Arthur. 1990. The systematics and evolution of subtribe Stenocereinae. 8. Organ pipe cactus and its closest relatives. *Cactus and Succulent Journal (U.S.)*. 62:13–24.

Gibson, Arthur, and Park Nobel. 1986. *The Cactus Primer*. Cambridge, Mass.: Harvard University Press.

Gibson, Arthur, and K. Norak. 1978. Systematic anatomy and phylogeny of Mexican columnar cacti. *Annals of the Missouri Botanical Gardens* 65:999–1057.

Hastings, J. Rodney, and Ray W. Turner. 1965. *The Changing Mile*. Tucson: University of Arizona Press.

Hodgson, W. 2001. *Food Plants of the Sonoran Desert*. Tucson: University of Arizona Press.

López Pérez, Joel. 1999. La pitaya maresmeña (*Stenocereus thurberi*) en el estado de Sinaloa. In Eulogio Pimienta-Barrios, editor, *El pitayo en Jalisco y especies afines en México*, 172–86. Guadalajara: Universidad de Guadalajara.

Martin, Paul S., David Yetman, Mark Fishbein, Phil Jenkins, Thomas R. Van Devender, and Rebecca Wilson, editors. 1998. *Gentry's Río Mayo Plants: The Tropical Deciduous Forest and Environs of Northwest Mexico*. Tucson: University of Arizona Press.

Naranjo, María Elena, Carlos Rengifo, and Pascual J. Soriano. 2003. Effect of ingestion by bats and birds on seed germination of *Stenocereus griseus* and *Subpilocereus repandus* (Cactaceae). *Journal of Tropical Biology* 19:19–25.

Obregón, Baltazar. 1584. *Historia de los descubrimientos de Nueva España*. New edition, 1997. Sevilla: Ediciones Alfar.

Och, Joseph. 1965. *Missionary in Sonora*. Edited by T. Treutlein. California Historical Society Special Publication no. 40.

Parker, Kathleen. 1987. Seedcrop characteristics and minimum reproductive size of organ pipe cactus (*Stenocereus thurberi*) in southern Arizona. *Madroño* 34:294–303.

———. 1988. Growth rates of *Stenocereus thurberi* and *Lophocereus schottii* in southern Arizona. *Botanical Gazette* 149:335–46.

Pennington, Campbell. 1980. *Vocabulario en la lengua*

Névome. Salt Lake City: University of Utah Press.

Pérez de Ribas, A. 1999. *History of the Triumphs of Our Holy Faith amongst the Most Barbarous and Fierce Peoples of the New World.* Translated by D. Reff, M. Ahern, and R. Danford. Tucson: University of Arizona Press.

Pfefferkorn, Ignaz. 1989. *Sonora: A Description of the Province.* Tucson: University of Arizona Press.

Rea, Amadeo. 1997. *At the Desert's Green Edge.* Tucson: University of Arizona Press.

Reina Guerrero, Ana Lilia. 1993. Contribución a la introducción de nuevos cultivos en Sonora: Las plantas medicinales de los Pimas Bajos del municipio de Yécora. Unpublished M.Sc. thesis, Universidad de Sonora.

Sahley, C. 2001. Vertebrate pollination, fruit production, and pollen dispersal of *Stenocereus thurberi* (Cactaceae). *The Southwest Naturalist* 46:261–71.

Shreve, Forrest, and Ira Wiggins. 1964. *Vegetation and Flora of the Sonoran Desert.* Palo Alto, Calif.: Stanford University Press.

Turner, R., J. Bowers, and T. Burgess. 1995. *Sonoran Desert Plants: An Ecological Atlas.* Tucson: University of Arizona Press.

Underhill, Ruth. 1946. *Papago Indian Religion.* New York: Columbia University Press.

Van Devender, T. R. 1987. Holocene vegetation and climate in the Puerto Blanco Mountains, southwestern Arizona. *Quaternary Research* 27:51–72.

———. 2002. History of the Sonoran Desert. In T. Fleming and A. Valiente-Banuet, editors, *Columnar Cacti and Their Mutualists*, 3–24. Tucson: University of Arizona Press.

Yetman, D., and T. R. Van Devender. 1991. The organ pipe cactus, *Stenocereus thurberi*: The distribution, morphology, and ethnobotany of pitahayas. *Haseltonia* 8:30–36.

———. 2002. *Mayo Ethnobotany: Land, History, and Traditional Knowledge in Northwest Mexico.* Berkeley: University of California Press.

Index

About the Author

DAVID YETMAN is research social scientist at the Southwest Center of The University of Arizona. The author of numerous books and articles, Yetman has specialized in studying the people and land of northwestern Mexico and has published books on Guarijíos, Mayos, and Seris. By his own admission he is a cactophile, one inordinately fond of cacti. He has lived in the Sonoran Desert since 1961. A former Pima County Supervisor, Yetman holds a Ph.D. in philosophy from The University of Arizona. He is the host for the television documentary series *The Desert Speaks,* produced by KUAT Television in Tucson and distributed by American Public Television. He lives in Tucson in a home surrounded by cacti.

The Southwest Center Series   Joseph C. Wilder, Editor